BUT I'M BORED!

BUT I'M BORED!

Discover the Power of Independent Play
to Raise Confident, Resilient Kids

Lizzie Assa, MSEd

Founder of The Workspace for Children

G. P. PUTNAM'S SONS
NEW YORK

PUTNAM
— EST. 1838 —

G. P. PUTNAM'S SONS

Publishers Since 1838

an imprint of Penguin Random House LLC

1745 Broadway, New York, NY 10019

penguinrandomhouse.com

Book design by Laura K. Corless

Library of Congress Cataloging-in-Publication Data

Names: Assa, Lizzie, author.
Title: But I'm bored!: discover the power of independent play to raise confident, resilient kids / by Lizzie Assa, MSEd, Founder of the Workspace for Children.
Description: New York: G. P. Putnam's Sons, [2026] |
Includes bibliographical references and index.
Identifiers: LCCN 2025005150 (print) | LCCN 2025005151 (ebook) |
ISBN 9798217043996 (hardcover) | ISBN 9798217044009 (ebook)
Subjects: LCSH: Play. | Active learning. | Early childhood education.
Classification: LCC LB1139.35.P55 A88 2026 (print) |
LCC LB1139.35.P55 (ebook) | DDC 649/.5—dc23/eng/20250225
LC record available at https://lccn.loc.gov/2025005150
LC ebook record available at https://lccn.loc.gov/2025005151

Printed in the United States of America
1st Printing

The authorized representative in the EU for product safety and compliance is Penguin Random House Ireland, Morrison Chambers, 32 Nassau Street, Dublin D02 YH68, Ireland, https://eu-contact.penguin.ie.

For Nate, Ruby, and Sloane.
Being your mom is the greatest honor of my life.
And to Dave, who always believed in me.

CONTENTS

BUT I'M BORED!

PLAY MORE, STRESS LESS

Parenting is overwhelming. Let's just admit that. No matter what you might see online or read in books, most parents are running around like crazy, feeling like they never get it all done or do any of it exactly right. Is your home in a constant state of chaos and clutter? Are you burned out? Are you ever able to concentrate on just one thing? Do you feel like your only job is to feed, clean, and entertain your child? Does a nap sound like an impossible dream? Whether you have an infant or a preteen, one child or six children, chances are you sometimes secretly feel like you're barely getting by.

Parents are expected to do it all—work full-time while also parenting perfectly, or if they stay at home with their kids, control every aspect of their children's development to make sure they turn into baby geniuses. There's a lot of noise in the parenting space today. Just look at Instagram. It's filled with influencers suggesting that if you don't parent this way or that way, or if you fail to maintain a certain high level of engagement with your kids, or stimulate them with enough learning, you're doing it wrong. The implication is that you might be a bad parent and your child will suffer because of it.

Kids feel overwhelmed, too. They don't always know what they're supposed to be doing, and that can make them feel unsteady. Unsteady feelings can lead to unwanted behaviors. They can't always articulate their likes and dislikes, or fully display their natural talents. They don't always know how to ask for help when they don't understand something. Depending on their developmental stage, they may have trouble expressing their emotions, following rules, or connecting with you in the way you wish they could. That can cause anxiety and undermine self-confidence in them and you. At home, children crave connection, and they want to show you what they can do, but they don't always know how to get your attention, especially if you are too stressed or overwhelmed to offer it. At the same time, they long for more independence and some control over their own lives. What's a conflicted, confused, stressed-out parent to do?

You'll begin to find the answers with independent play.

In all the press I have done over the years, no matter who is interviewing me, I get the same question again and again, which is some form of: "How do I get my children to play independently?" As the founder of The Workspace for Children, I have real, practical, simple, low-effort, high-impact answers to that question. Teaching parents and children how to institute independent play successfully in their homes is my mission. I have an MSEd from the Bank Street College of Education in New York City and have taught at the Downtown Little School and the City and Country School in Manhattan, where child-led play principles are prized and practiced.

Independent play has multiple benefits, including giving parents some time to themselves and building confidence and creativity in their children. This book will help you to create a home environment conducive to independent play. My goal is to help you personalize independent play for your unique family and child. The strategies I teach work, and I know that because I've used them with the many families I've coached, as well as with my own children.

There is a lot of noise in the parenting space these days. When I decided to write this book, I did not want to add to all the noise. I wanted to help turn down the noise. If you follow parenting influencers, it can be difficult not to feel the pressure to be a perfect parent. You don't have to do everything perfectly. It's possible to get clear on what your family values are and create a life that reflects them. You can help your child to feel safe, connected, comfortable, and confident at home, even if the outside world doesn't always feel that way. In the process, you'll free your child to be a child, and create more time for yourself. You'll be better able to meet your own needs and parent in a way that feels more authentic to who you are. No perfection required.

When children play independently, they get to explore their lives and inner world on their own, instead of following someone else's direction. They learn to come up with their own ideas, instead of relying on *your* ideas. They learn to make plans, create what they imagine, figure out who they are and what they really love to do. Independent playtime will give your children the opportunity to explore their own thoughts and interests.

You may be in the habit of preventing your child from becoming bored, but boredom is exactly what opens the door for children to begin dreaming, creating, and gaining confidence in their own ability to entertain themselves.

Even if, for you, your child playing independently just means you finally get a chance to clean up the kitchen without anybody pulling on your clothing or whining "Mooommm" or "Daaaddd," wouldn't that be worth the time it takes to read this book? You can have this. Your family can have this. This book was designed for you.

The goal of my work, my business, my courses, and now this book, is to build play confidence in ways that contribute to the culture of your family. In this book, you'll learn more about how to discover who your child really is, what's developmentally appropriate, how to think differently about what play is, and how your child could best be playing independently, in a way tailored to their unique personality.

You'll learn how to create play pockets throughout your home, how to choose open-ended toys that spark imagination rather than controlling it, how to set play boundaries and stick to them, the wonders of quiet time, and how to close the loop afterward with connection time that strengthens your relationship with your child, helps them to feel seen and loved, and doesn't take up your entire day.

I'm also going to talk frankly about parental guilt, because not spending time with your children can feel like you aren't doing your job. In reality, it's exactly the opposite. I know what parental burnout feels like. I've been there myself. Time to yourself will ultimately make you more emotionally available to your children.

If somebody told me to read a book about a parenting system that was going to take a lot of time and be a lot of work, I wouldn't be interested. That's not the book I'm writing. These strategies aren't about giving you more to do. They are about giving you less to do, with high-impact, low-effort strategies that will give you the space and time you need to replenish and get things done that aren't about direct interaction with your children. Then, when you are with your child, you will be a more connected, more alert, more focused, better-listening parent than you were before.

That's what every child really needs.

In a world we can't always control, independent play gives children the chance to create a world they *can* control. As you watch your child become more independent, more confident at expressing their natural talents, and more self-directed, and as you see their interests sprouting and spreading from the seeds you have planted at home, your entire family will benefit. You will all feel calmer, more connected, and your child won't depend on you—or on screens—for their constant entertainment.

This book will help you to create an oasis of calm in your home where your family can be together and—in ways *everybody* loves and needs—also be apart.

1

My Path to Play

I wasn't always a play expert, although I was fortunate enough to grow up in a play-rich environment. I'm one of five children, the second oldest. I grew up in the '80s, when parents told their kids to "go outside and play," no arguments. My mom was one of those parents. She rarely played with us, but she created a home environment where my siblings and I were expected to play together.

In our kitchen, there was a long, child-height art table where we sat for hours sorting through the drawers of stickers, coloring elaborate pictures, while laughing, fighting, and creating. Downstairs in the playroom, we had ample space to wrestle, play pretend with dolls and stuffed animals, and build elaborate block structures. When we inevitably got too loud, she'd send us outside to the backyard where we had a playhouse, buckets of chalk, jump ropes, and bicycles.

Play rebuilt my self-esteem. My school days were filled with stomachaches and worry, but when I was playing with my siblings or friends, I felt safe, interesting, and creative. Play gave me what school didn't: a sense of purpose and a sense of who I was and what I could do. At a very young age, play showed me that I could be relaxed and confident. Now I know, as an educator and independent play specialist, just how valuable creating opportunities for a child to play independently can be.

As I grew older, I reveled in helping to care for my younger siblings and the younger siblings of my friends. I became a babysitter, camp counselor, and often the leader in any playful or creative endeavors that arose. I felt especially drawn to the anxious child or the child who tended to "get in trouble" at school. I wanted to help children build confidence in themselves, so I decided to study education.

Once I got to college, I started to realize I wasn't so bad at school after all. My freshman year, I had a literal aha moment when I realized, *Wait, I'm not stupid!* I started paying attention and doing my work because I was finally studying things I cared about. Early childhood education became my passion.

When I was doing my student teaching, I begged them to let me stay with the kindergarten instead of moving to the upper grades. I was student teaching in lower Manhattan, in the four-year-old classroom, when the events of September 11 happened. When December rolled around, and it was time to move placements, we decided that I would stay in that classroom for the remainder of the school year. The children and families who lived in the surrounding area needed consistency. As a student myself, I was learning more about children and the healing power of play than I could have anywhere else. I am so grateful for that experience.

After graduate school, I worked in what I think was one of the best nursery schools in Manhattan, the Downtown Little School (now closed). "Play-Based Curriculum" is a buzzy catchphrase, and many programs claim it as their focus. Truth be told, for many programs, the "play-based" descriptor is inaccurate. When you dig a little deeper, you'll find that many of these programs are using a traditional, teacher-centered approach rather than a child-led play-based approach. But the Downtown Little School was, at its core, play-based and child-led. I remember our director explaining that "learning how to be at school" was the curriculum for the young twos: how to be away from their grown-ups, how to eat school snacks, put on their shoes, and when to try the potty. They didn't need to start memorizing letters and numbers and other developmentally inappropriate lessons.

Loris Malaguzzi, the founder of the Reggio Emilia Approach to early childhood education, which has influenced the curriculums of many preschools here and abroad, believed that the children are the curriculum. To me, that is the basis of a true child-led play-based learning experience.

After that, I worked at another well-known school called the City and Country School in Manhattan. The nursery program is a play-based, child-centered curriculum, focusing on social, emotional, and cognitive development. During my time at C&C, the children in my threes class worked with clay, paint, books, water, and blocks as their main materials for learning. I discovered a lot about play in my short time at City and Country.

Then I became pregnant with my oldest child and quickly embraced the role of full-time motherhood. Even before my first child was born, I was making plans to use what I'd learned in the early childhood classroom to set up a home environment that supported play. My years of working with children and families prepared me for success as a mom to small children. Of course, like most parents, I was exhausted from constant nighttime parenting, diaper changes, and car seat battles. But I also reveled in creating play environments for my kids, providing snacks and art experiences. I was less stressed about parenting small children than many of my friends with children the same ages. At first, I couldn't figure out why, and then it hit me—I was implementing systems that I had used in the early childhood settings to prepare my kids for independence and play.

When my youngest child was one, I opened a small studio in my basement for parents and young kids. I called it The Workspace for Children. I wanted to show parents and caregivers how to use play to encourage their children to be productive and independent. I engineered play activities for the little ones and talked to the adults about development and play, showing them what happens when you prepare an environment and trust your kids to play in it. I did this every Tuesday and Thursday, and it took off like wildfire. People were shocked to learn what was possible in the playroom. Nobody was doing this ten years ago. I outgrew my basement within a year.

Having people coming into our home to play, and the necessary mess that created, was stressful on my family life. I knew I didn't want to take a job outside of my home, so I closed the studio and transitioned The Workspace for Children to an online platform. I began to share the work that transpired in the play studio, along with play ideas I was doing with my children. I shared teacher tips, which turned into parenting advice that was working in my own home. My Instagram account (@theworkspaceforchildren) quickly took off, so I began writing a weekly blog about parenting and play.

My blog readership and IG audience grew exponentially. To support our family's income, I began to consult for a local childcare program that was opening as part of a coworking space. Then, people began to hire me to come into their homes and set up play spaces. One of my more popular blog posts is about how to build an outdoor tinker space for your kids. I used to build one every spring for my children, and then people began hiring me to build them in backyards all over town.

The more I saw the impact of what I was sharing, the more I understood how important teaching people about independent play really is. Play impacts not only the child and their future development and growth, but the entire family dynamic and the experience of parenting.

About This Book

Over the years, many have approached me to write a book. I always said no because I didn't have the bandwidth, and I felt that people were overwhelmed by too much online parenting advice—I didn't want to add to it. I'm so glad Instagram didn't exist yet when I was a new mom. It would have sent me into the deep end. There are so many people on Instagram telling you all the things that are right and wrong. I didn't want to tell people what to do or judge how they raised their children, so writing a book really wasn't on my radar.

But the more I followed what was going on in the parenting space, the more I thought that maybe people need a book like this. My mission is different. I want to support parents and caregivers by helping them make small tweaks and changes so that their parenting feels more aligned with their values and goals. You'll never hear me say, "This is exactly how you should do XYZ." I want to help people adjust their parenting with tweaks according to what's authentic to them. I don't want to say, "Do it this way!" with the implication that if you don't, you're doing it all wrong.

Finally, I decided that I would write a book if it could *turn down the noise.* That's why customizing independent play for *your* family and *your* unique child is so important to me. You don't have to parent the way I parent. I want you to parent how *you* parent, according to your values, but in a way that's informed by things you might not otherwise know. More than anything, I want to help parents of young children ease their anxiety about parenting and about trying to do it all and be perfect.

Every family has its challenges. I felt confident about my parenting when my kids were little, but now that those kids are teens, I finally understand what it feels like to be an anxious parent! I have a whole new understanding of how parents feel when they have a toddler and don't know what to do! Now, when *I* say to people, "I don't know what to do!" they look at me funny and say, "Yeah, so? I haven't known what to do for fifteen years!"

I'm still learning, as we all are, but what this book can do for you and your family is to take the pressure off so you can help your kids grow and become more themselves through the power of play. In a world that we can't control, for our kids or for ourselves, play gives children the opportunity to create a world that they *can* influence and shape.

Are you ready to try this? Great. Then I have three words for you:

"Let them play."

PART ONE

1

"BUT I'M BORED!"

"But I'm bored!"

How tempting it is, when our children whine those three dreaded words, to tell them to "Just go play." Isn't that what children are supposed to do? Play? But it's too hard, or they won't, or they can't.

People roll their eyes when I suggest that children need more time to practice playing. They tell me that when they were kids, they played in the woods all afternoon. No one even checked on them, let alone taught them how to play. And the parents certainly didn't play with their kids all day. Parents didn't see it as their job to play, at least not all the time.

If you were a kid in the 1980s or '90s, you had the time to get bored, come up with your own ideas, and see them through. Do you remember the freedom you felt playing on your own, creating imaginary worlds, acting out fantastic stories with your stuffed animals or dolls, drawing or reading or writing stories, jumping rope or drawing hopscotch boards on the sidewalk with chalk, inventing games and riding your bike around the neighborhood? It's likely that when you were a kid, you had all the time in the world to play independently, so you got really good at it.

There were flaws in that system, certainly—parents were often less connected with their kids than they are today, less aware of what was going on in their lives. They didn't always fully grasp their children's unique skills and problems. Although there were obvious exceptions, a fond but nonchalant disregard for the child's world was just the way parents were in that cultural moment, for better or for worse.

Today, that kind of parenting attitude feels impossible, even neglectful. The world seems a lot less safe, which naturally puts parents on high alert. We worry more, we think about our kids more, and we are a lot more *interested* in our kids than parents used to be, or so it seems to me. We want to know everything about our kids. They amaze us. We marvel at who they are becoming, and we want all the details about what they're doing in school, who their friends are, what they're thinking about, what they struggle with, who they are. I certainly feel that way about my kids, and I bet you do, too.

However, somewhere along the line, the beautiful and necessary attachment between parents and children has seeped into the realm of play, and that's not such a good thing. Many kids don't know how to play by themselves anymore. Busy schedules, on-demand screens, and parental pressure to entertain kids are all important factors. Most of us feel like we should be interacting with our children at every opportunity, leaving us overwhelmed. And let's just admit right now that irritation can lurk just under the surface, too—especially when the children beg for one more game, one more story, or just five more minutes. I get that.

But here's the encouraging part: Children inherently know how to play, even if they've forgotten, or gotten out of the habit, or don't get the chance to exercise that inherent gift very often so far. There is value and beauty in what children do naturally. Wouldn't you love to see your child's self-confidence bloom? Wouldn't it be amazing if your kids felt like autonomous family members who contributed willingly and happily in support of the family and the household? Wouldn't it be amazing if they felt so safely connected to you that they had no problem going into their own rooms and playing quietly for an hour or more? What if your kids loved to do their own "work" nearby, when you do yours, without you having to direct their process? I've seen it happen, hundreds of times, in families who never thought their child would play without direction.

All of this can come out of an independent play routine.

Time alone can replenish everyone, so that family togetherness becomes the reward and the payoff, rather than another stressor. What would you do with that time? How much less stress would you feel? How happy would you be to reconnect with your children afterward, to learn what they did, what they dreamed, what they built, and to see how excited they are to show you?

Who we are alone is someone different from who we are with others, and knowing both those parts of yourself is valuable for everyone's growth. Until they are alone, a child may not be able to distinguish their own needs and desires from someone else's. Does your middle child know who she is without her big sister directing the show? Does your youngest son know who he is when you aren't guiding all his activities? Do you know who you are when you aren't in the throes of parenting?

Just to be clear, spending together time with your child is *essential* for a loving and secure connection. I highly recommend it—but not 24-7. In fact, constant together time is counterproductive for parents, for children, and for the relationship between them. There are many effective ways to *connect* without pretend-playing with your child all the time (more on that later). The secret to a more harmonious family life is a balance of connection and independent play.

In this book, I'm going to help you find that balance. We can reclaim the beneficial parts of the independent play we knew when we were young, while still building secure, connected relationships between parents and children. Reclaiming your child's independence in play and unlearning what you thought was your role in their play is the answer.

It is less complicated than you might think. You'll be surprised, once you get started, by what independent play can do for your family dynamic, your parental stress level, and your child's confidence and creativity.

Embracing Boredom

Let's talk about boredom. We all want kids who can self-start and play well independently, but when they start to complain about boredom, it can feel like a five-alarm fire we need to put out right away.

Close your eyes and picture yourself in that moment when your child whines, "But I'm bored!" What are you feeling right now? Irritated? Guilty? Anxious? Fearful that if you don't give your children something to do, they'll destroy the house, get in trouble, zone out on screens, or at least make a huge mess that you know *you'll* probably end up cleaning because it's easier than trying to force them to do it? (Been there.)

It can feel like your child's boredom is a sign that you aren't doing enough as a parent. Shouldn't you be teaching them something, spending "quality time" with them, providing them with stimulating materials that will make them smarter, more creative, demonstrate good values, increase their social skills, and turn them into model citizens? (Just saying all that makes me anxious.) And shouldn't you be keeping them off screens?

Headlines about the state of childhood in a digital world, and compelling but frightening books like *The Anxious Generation*, have left many parents feeling fearful and frozen when considering how much time their children may spend on screens. We know we need to reinsert unstructured play back into our children's lives, but they are accustomed to the instant gratification of their digital world. They are used to being entertained by their screens, so if we say no, what happens? They want us to entertain them. Then we feel guilty. After all, if we're taking away screens, we should play with our kids, right?

I'll talk about screens more later, but for now, it is time to let go of the stress and confusion. I can save you some time by telling you that entertaining your children all day every day leads to burnout for you and a child who relies on external sources for entertainment.

Boredom is important for your child. A child who never gets bored misses a powerful opportunity to develop creativity.

The value of boredom is becoming more recognized. A *New York Times* headline published during the pandemic quarantine was: "How to Entertain Your Kids This Summer? Maybe Don't." Another *NYT* article around the same time encouraged parents to begin teaching their children independent play.

Yes, boredom is beneficial. Here's what it helps kids do:

1. **Develop self-reliance.** Boredom teaches your child to make real-time decisions and become less reliant on constant entertainment. Being comfortable with boredom wires your child to look inward instead of outward.

2. **Discover personal interests.** When children have the consistent opportunity to get bored, come up with an idea, and follow through, they learn what truly interests them and gain the confidence to pursue those interests.

3. **Optimize brain development.** Boredom provides essential brain breaks, preventing meltdowns and irritability, and allowing for optimal brain development.

4. **Learn mindfulness.** Learning to embrace downtime helps children become mindful and comfortable with their own thoughts. As adults, we spend hundreds of dollars on apps, supplements, and classes that promise to help us be more mindful. Embracing boredom and committing to downtime for your children will give them the break they need without the price tag attached.

5. **Improve perseverance.** Children who come up with their own ideas are more motivated to find answers and persevere through challenges. Encouraging children to ask questions and explore their curiosities helps foster intrinsic motivation, problem-solving skills, and resilience.

6. **Hone decision-making skills.** Decision-making is a muscle that needs exercise. Boredom provides the practice needed to strengthen this skill. Allowing children to be bored, rather than constantly providing entertainment, gives them opportunities to make choices, take initiative, and develop their decision-making abilities.

But . . . can we really do it? Let our children be bored? Won't there be an uprising? How do you even start?

You may have heard that you should just "let your kids be bored," and a lot of parents will respond, "No way, I'm not doing that, they'll destroy the house." First, let's make an important dis-tinction: *There is a difference between productive boredom and destructive boredom,* and your approach matters. Your child's disruptive or destructive behavior is a signal that they need your support. The most effective way to support your child is with con-nection. Your child is getting your attention one way or another way. You get to choose whether you give them that attention in a productive, supportive way, or by yelling and getting angry.

In other words, children need to be bored, but with support. This is not ignoring your child. It is holding intentional space for them to get innovative. For example, my eleven-year-old still comes into my home office, rolls her eyes, and says, "Mom, I'm so bored, can I watch a show?" Every single time it makes me laugh to myself. I usually hug her and answer her with some version of, "Nope. You can't. Go be bored somewhere other than my office."

How can I say that so flippantly? Because, most days, I've spent some time connecting with her before heading into my office to work. Also, our home environment is set up for her to play, make, and create, so I'm able to confidently let her figure it out. I know that she has everything she needs to be productively bored, and I have a plan to connect with her after I'm done with my work.

It's revelatory to realize that nothing is wrong with your child or you and that you have the power to shift how your child con-tends with boredom.

The Remedy for Guilt Is Connection

I think it's safe to assume that all parents feel guilty sometimes. Am I doing enough for my kids? Too much? Am I doing a good job? Unfortunately, guilt is part of being a parent. Rationally, you might know that it's important to take a break from entertaining your child constantly, but the guilt keeps you on the hamster wheel.

Even when parents successfully embrace independent play as part of their family's culture, they often tell me some version of, "Lizzie, I followed your programs, and my child *loves* independent play! They have quiet time every day and want more! I know I should be happy about this, but now that they're busy playing, I suddenly feel guilty."

The remedy for guilt is connection. When you connect with your child in meaningful ways throughout the day, you'll start to feel really good about the fact that they know how to play independently.

Connection has become somewhat of a buzzword, and maybe you're tired of hearing about how connection is a parenting cure-all. It is and it isn't. First, let's define what connection isn't. Connection is *not* pretending to play with your child while scrolling through your phone. It's not giving your child a bath while running in and out of the room. It's not moving game pieces in Monopoly while texting. If you're multitasking, you're not paying attention, and that is when they keep saying, "Play with me! Play with me!" And you think, "I can never fill their bucket!" The problem is you are giving them half your attention, and they want it all.

But, if you give your child undivided attention, won't they just want more, more, more, and the problem of entertaining them will get worse? What if they never let you get back to what you need to be doing? This may happen at first, but the truth is that once you start connecting consistently, your child will actually need less and less from you. The more they feel fulfilled by your undivided attention, the less effort they will spend on attention-seeking.

Your child will thrive as they become more independent. However, they won't love independent play if it's only something they are sent away to do when you're busy. They learn to love it when it's part of a predictable routine that includes a connection with a trusted grown-up. Just fifteen minutes of completely focused time doing something together, even if it is just talking, listening, or cuddling, can do the trick.

Think about this: When do you feel most connected to your partner? Is it at a loud happy hour where you're together but constantly interrupted? Or is it on a peaceful morning walk with no distractions? Close your eyes for a moment and reflect. What do you need from someone to feel seen, heard, and understood? When you receive that, how does it make you feel?

Adults know that connections are made by learning more about the other person. People want to feel heard. That's how you get to know someone, create trust, and build relationships. Kids respond to that same level of interest and respect, and it makes their independent playtime all the more fruitful, knowing they get to report back to you afterward—and that you will be refreshed enough to really listen.

Exercises to Respond to Your Child's Boredom

Before we move on to more detailed information about how to personalize independent play for your child, I've got some exercises for you to try. Let's say your toddler is napping, and your kindergartner approaches you, whining, "I'm bored!" Here's what you can do:

Step 1: Check in with yourself. When you hear that your child is bored, do you feel fear, guilt, or resentment? Take a deep breath, and remind yourself that all children get bored. It's normal and expected. It's not your fault, and it's not their fault, either.

Step 2: Respond, don't react. Once you feel calm, you can respond more effectively. Follow these steps to decide whether your child needs your immediate attention or can handle their boredom.

1. **Have you connected today?**

   If yes, your child doesn't need you to stop and entertain them. Say, "I hear you. You're bored. It's okay to be bored."

   If no, spend a few moments connecting. Say, "We haven't really had a chance to hang out today, have we? Let's set a timer for fifteen minutes and work on your puzzle. After that, you can find something to do while I get back to my emails."

2. **What are your child's immediate needs?** Is your child truly bored, or are they actually hungry, tired, lonely, or needing to expend some energy? Address the underlying need:

   Tired: "You're telling me you're bored. I wonder if you're tired. The garbage trucks woke you up early this morning. I bet your stuffies are tired, too. Let's tuck them in and you can read them some books in bed."

   Lonely: "You're telling me you're bored. I wonder if you're feeling lonely. Let's text your uncle and set up a time to read together on FaceTime. Would you like some supplies to make cards for your cousins? Let's find out when they can play."

Restless: *"I see your body jiggling and wiggling. Maybe playing on your scooter is a good idea?"*

Hungry: *"You're having a hard time figuring out what to do. It's almost time for a snack. Let's have something to eat and figure it out together."*

3. **Empower them.** If their basic needs are met, say, "I hear you. You're not sure what to do with yourself right now. It's different from when I help you build a castle. We can do that together after lunch. Right now, you get to decide how to spend your time. I wonder if you will read a book or color." This approach tells your child when they will connect with you next, and shows that you understand their feelings, while having confidence in their ability to manage boredom.

It's perfectly okay if you've parented one way and now want to make an adjustment. You may also find some of the approaches in this book work for you and others don't. Choose what works. This is not about all-or-nothing. Select the strategies that resonate and make sense to you, and let go of the rest. You may come back to other strategies later. Adapt what fits your family and your style right now. Embrace the process.

Let's end with a few more prompts for responding to your child's boredom.

Scenario: Your child says, "My brothers are playing without me, and they won't let me play."

You can say: "Your brothers are playing a game for older kids.

I bet you feel really left out. It's hard to feel that way. Tell me more about what's happening."

It's tempting to intervene, make the brothers play with their sister, or offer a list of activities and toys. Resist that urge. Your child needs to feel heard and understood more than they need a solution from you. They want to feel strong and capable, with your support as their anchor.

Scenario: Your child says, "I have no one to play with."

You can say: "You wish you had someone to play with. I hear you. If you could play with anyone right now, who would that be? Tell me about it."

Resist the urge to list all their recent playdates or remind them of the time you spent together this morning. They need to feel heard, not reminded.

Scenario: "There's nothing to do."

You can say: "Sounds like you don't know what to do next, and that doesn't feel great right now."

In this situation, just listen neutrally. As they talk and feel heard, they will likely come up with an idea themselves.

Note: Use these scripts as sample conversations, not lines to memorize. Respond in ways authentic to you and your child. I only give you these examples to get you started on how to think about the impact of your responses to your child's boredom.

Don't expect an overnight transformation in your family. There is a learning curve. If your child was learning how to read, you wouldn't expect them to dive straight into a Harry Potter book by themselves. You would start with short, easy readers. You would expect the process to take time, practice, resources, and support. Managing boredom is the same.

Celebrate the small wins. It's going to get better. By connecting with your child and supporting them through boredom without fixing it for them, you're helping them develop crucial life skills. I'm here with you every step of the way. It doesn't mean the big waves aren't going to crash over your head, because sometimes they will, but with connection and independent play, you'll have an anchor to hold on to until the waves recede, and you will remain aligned with your family values.

2

UNDERSTANDING
YOUR UNIQUE CHILD

A s a parent, you know your child better than anyone else. You know what will set them off and exactly how to comfort them when they're scared in the middle of the night. You know what angle they like their sandwich cut and which sweater is too itchy to wear to preschool. You know your child better than the pediatrician, their teacher, and a lot better than the influencer telling you all the things you "should" be doing or not doing.

I want to help you use what you already know about your unique child to open doors to parts of your child that you might not have noticed before. When you start to intentionally observe your child, you will see them in new and distinct ways, not just as someone you love and are responsible for, but as a truly capable person with highly developed preferences, opinions, and qualities. When you begin to explore their interests and capabilities, you will become uniquely qualified to help them start working on their own projects and thinking about the world in their own way, rather than through your filter.

"What Did You Want Me to Notice?"

As parents, we play the role of director. We are so entrenched in fulfilling our kids' basic needs—making sure they are fed, changed, read to, and asleep on time—that we often forget to step back and think about who they *are* . . . and who they are becoming. Taking time to intentionally observe our children, especially in play, is a direct window into the inner workings of their minds. Creating a habit of observation and narration makes a remarkable difference in how we respond to our children and how they move through the world.

Observation is a powerful tool. Saying, "Did you want me to notice that . . ." is to dig deeper into any interactions you might have with a child. Letting a child know you are noticing what they are doing can make them feel important and open up new avenues for communication and learning about who they are and what matters to them.

I'm thinking of a little four-year-old wearing a new dinosaur shirt. They walk into the room and look so excited. A typical response as adults is to say, "Oh, I love your shirt! You must really like dinosaurs," and that's the end of the conversation. It doesn't really leave anything for the child to say. However, if you continue the interaction and go a little deeper, you can get more out of them in a way that is reinforcing for their confidence and verbal skills.

You might say, "It looks like you want me to notice that shirt. You're kind of holding your shoulders back so I can see your shirt really well."

They might say, "Yeah, this is my dinosaur shirt. My nana got it for me."

You can continue to be curious and open a whole conversation, whether it's about dinosaurs or shirts or Nana, by asking open-ended questions and listening to which direction the child wants to go. Maybe they weren't trying to get you to notice the shirt at all, but instead, were really trying to get you to notice something else. "Did you want me to notice . . ." shows the child that you truly see them for who they are, rather than them being just like any other four-year-old. It builds deeper connections and invites more opportunities for child-led conversation.

Imagine being on the playground where a group of preschoolers are playing. Two children are negotiating for a bucket, one grabbing from the other. The child who is empty-handed looks up expectantly for a grown-up to help them navigate the situation. They cry in the direction of the teacher. The teacher notices and approaches the children. She jumps in and stops the more dominant child from grabbing. She admonishes the grabber and gives the bucket to the whimpering child.

Or, the teacher approaches and says to the whimpering child, "Your face looks upset and I see that you keep looking at me. Did you want me to notice that you need some help? You can say, 'Teacher! I need help!'" Then the teacher bends down and asks what's happening, allowing the children to each explain. She might say, "Hmm, I wonder what we can do here. You want that bucket, and Sam seems to want that bucket, too." Then she pauses thoughtfully. In this second scenario, the teacher doesn't assume she knows what the children's point of view is. Instead, she opens the conversation and invites them to lead the dialogue as she supports them.

Asking children if they want you to notice something builds emotional intelligence skills, as they learn to verbalize what they want or need. You can learn so much more from children by getting curious about their intentions than you can if you think you already know what they are. But first, you have to notice that they want you to notice. This is where observation comes in.

Let's look at some of the ways you can begin to notice aspects of your child through the lens of personality and development, and how that specifically can inform the way your child plays.

There are four categories related to personality and development that I have found particularly useful for intentionally observing your child: strengths, challenges, emotional life, and personal interests. Let's start with your child's strengths.

Noticing Their Strengths

Even your tiny baby has traits and abilities that help them do things successfully. For example, your baby might be physically strong, making feeding and releasing gas easier. Your baby might have a high frustration tolerance. They may be determined to roll, and even if it's difficult, they keep at it until they turn over. You might have a child who is not easily stimulated by noise or light and can fall asleep easily, resulting in a well-rested baby and a relaxed parent.

Think about your own child's strengths. Some of the strengths children at different ages and stages might have include being particularly verbal; having a long attention span; being easygoing and friendly; adapting well to new environments; trying new things; being curious, independent, or an adventurer; climbing and doing somersaults and cartwheels; or being particularly tuned into emotions, displaying empathy.

Every child has strengths. Take just a little time to think about your child's strengths and write them down. Don't think too hard about this—what comes to mind right away? You are going to play to these strengths and use them to your advantage and to your child's advantage when thinking about how to establish opportunities for building confidence and independent play skills.

Noticing Their Challenges

Just as every child has strengths, every child has certain challenges. Challenges can encompass a wide range of situations and usually involve overcoming some kind of obstacle. What challenges your child? Is your infant sensitive, waking up often and crying frequently? Is your three-year-old easily startled or scared by loud noises? Does your five-year-old have a hard time sitting still for more than a few moments in situations where it's required? Does your six-year-old balk at meeting new people? Does your eight-year-old feel challenged by age-appropriate reading or math?

When I call them challenges, I simply mean that they may cause your child discomfort in certain situations, especially if they (or an adult) compare themselves with other children who don't feel challenged in those areas (but certainly feel challenged in other areas). Knowing where your child feels challenged can help you to tailor independent play opportunities, during which your child can gain confidence and you can support them in a safe and personal way.

Again, don't overthink this. Make a list of a few things that come to mind, and keep it for reference. If you are having some trouble thinking of what to list here, you might work on this with your partner or a friend: What do you see as your child's strengths, and what do they see? What do you see as your child's challenges, and what do they see? You may be surprised that your lists have some interesting differences.

Noticing Their Emotional Life

No matter what developmental stage your child is in, you can always pay attention to what is happening for your child emotionally *right now*. Is there a new sibling, or a baby sibling that has recently become mobile and thus, more of a presence in your home? Has your little one recently met any developmental milestones, such as walking, balancing on one foot, or starting preschool? Have you moved into a new home or has a good friend of your child's moved away?

Many things have an impact on a child's emotions, even if they don't seem like a big deal to adults. Children are working so hard to assimilate new things in their lives that often, simple things they've been managing all along will regress. When you notice regression in your child, like a lapse in potty training, or a recurrence of night wakings, ask yourself what's new. Being able to identify that for yourself will help you feel a lot more in control and so much more patient.

The milestones I mentioned are fairly obvious, so I want to dig a little deeper. Let's think about some more subtle developments that can be happening with your child emotionally that can pack a huge punch. Your three-year-old or four-year-old might be working hard on taking turns at school. At home, they might need a break from sharing. Paying attention to this development will allow you to say, "I know how hard you are working on turn-taking at school. You can take this toy to your room to use it all by yourself during quiet time. You don't have to share with anyone." Knowing your child is mastering turn-taking will allow you to cheer them on in an authentic way and meet them where they are in their learning, rather than feeling irritated or confused as to why they are being selfish.

Here's another example: Your preschooler is working hard on

controlling impulses. Rather than getting angry when they reach out and push a friend at the park, you can anticipate that their impulse control is hot in the brain right now. You can say, "I'm going to stay near you to help," because you know that your child's mind and body are still learning to work together to think before grabbing or pushing. Your child will feel so supported and taken care of if you can express that you are on the same team, rather than an authority figure who doesn't understand their struggle and is angry. They will feel more connected to you, and less like they need your attention every second.

Maybe your child is a bit older. Your five- or six-year-old might be really interested in the behavior of her classmates or friends. They might be trying things on at home, in their safe place. Be really aware of this stage. Tell them you know that five- or six-year-olds are learning about how to act from their friends and classmates. You can allow them to baby talk or try new voices and actions, and still place a limit on it when necessary. "Your voice reminds me so much of what Cooper sounds like when he is feeling powerful! What does it feel like for you when *you* use that voice?" Also, "Friends can still be friends, even if they have different ideas/clothes/foods at lunchtime." Then illustrate that with an example from your own child's life that they already know to be true.

Children are still figuring out who they are and who they want to be. They are rediscovering their sense of self and what it means to assert it. Yes, they did this in their younger years, but now it has a much savvier spin to it, and you can be there to help them navigate this shift. Knowing what they are going through emotionally will allow you to connect with them on a much deeper level. When you train your parent brain to be in tune to your child's social and emotional state, you will find ways to connect the dots for them during their independent playtime.

Noticing Their Personal Interests

This is the most personalized category in this chapter, and the most frequently changing. What is your child mesmerized by right now? What do they get excited about when they look out the window of a car? What do they reach for when you are shopping or going for a walk? What do they suddenly start talking about a lot or asking questions about? Pay close attention to your child's interests. They are a major clue for how to set up play areas and cue independent play.

For example, if your toddler loves trucks or big loud vehicles, you know that tuning in to those monster machines is the way to their heart—at least, this week. If you pretend to drive the city bus to the bathroom, it may get your child there much faster than nagging them to hurry up before they have an accident. If your child is waiting with you in the doctor's office, bring along a few small vehicles to keep them occupied.

A personal example: My daughter was interested in taking care of babies. For her, we provided dolls, visited friends with newborns, read lots of books about babies, and carefully dressed and swaddled her favorite doll for the park. When she was struggling with separation anxiety or a trip to the doctor, we practiced on her dolls. I bought zillions of dollar store Band-Aids for her to put on her dolly's boo-boos, and we kept a real preemie pack of diapers around for her to play with. As she grew, her interests changed and so did the materials for her play.

Consider two five-year-olds I know. These are children of parents I've worked with who wanted my help setting up play spaces within their homes. These two children lived in similar environments but had very different personalities.

The first child was interested in art, and she loved to create things. She had a little brother, and it was important to her that she have a personal space with boundaries that would keep him from getting into her things. We set up an art space in the kitchen that was up higher than the art shelves that were open for everyone. She could get a little step stool and climb up there to get glue, scissors, and other supplies that weren't toddler-friendly. When her brother was napping, that's where she would go for her quiet time. She would sit at her table and create things with all the materials she really couldn't use around her little brother.

She was also really into horses, so we added open-ended materials that could feed her interest in horses—horse stickers, yarn to make horsehair, different soft materials for collage. I had a feeling that if her area were set up for her to think about and create horses, it would really draw her in, and it did. There were a lot of layers going on here: her need for autonomy, her need to have a space she didn't have to share, her need to lean into her strengths, her emotional needs, and her personal interests.

During that same month, I worked with another client who had a five-year-old boy who was musically gifted. He had a dedicated playroom, but his parents wanted help knowing how to set it up so he would want to spend time in there. He already had a piano and a keyboard, so we designed the space around those. We added big hollow blocks he could use to build a stage for performing. We filled a shelf with books about music and about people who play the piano. We made a work area with staff paper (the kind you write music on) and pens so he could pretend he was writing his own music. We added card stock and markers because he liked to make tickets to his shows and paper to make programs he could hand out to his "audience."

If I had set up a music playroom for the little girl who loved art, or an art studio for the little boy who loved music, neither of them would have been particularly interested. Sure, maybe she would draw pictures on the paper instead of making it into programs, or maybe he would make programs in the art area. However, putting intentional thought around what would draw each individual child sparked both children to play independently more often.

The materials in these play areas were personal but open-ended. We didn't add kits to make specific projects or materials that were about doing one thing and then you're done, like "make this necklace" or "play this song on this preprogrammed guitar." Art supplies and music supplies, books and toys that lend them-

THE FLEXIBILITY OF OPEN-ENDED MATERIALS

I often use the term "open-ended" when referring to toys or other materials to get kids creating. What I mean by open-ended is materials that can be used in a lot of different ways. Open-ended materials can become anything. They meet children where they are, no matter their interests or developmental stage. Kids' interests often evolve, and their developmental stages are always changing. They decide what the materials become, rather than the materials deciding what the play will become.

Open-ended materials can include paper, markers, pencils, and paint; magnetic tiles and blocks in different sizes and shapes; fabric squares and yarn; colored stones, wooden disks, buttons, and sorting trays; different sizes of bowls, balls, rings, and tops; play dough, modeling clay, and sand; light tables, balance boards, and parachute fabric; even household objects like pots and pans, wooden spoons, pillows, blankets, flashlights, and tools. Even water and some different sizes of cups, pitchers, and other containers can keep a child busy for a long time.

selves to a child's imagination, are more effective because they don't back you into a corner.

As you go about your day with your child, start to notice things using these different perspectives. You may begin to see your child in new ways and better understand the nuances of their behavior and preferences. Now let's add another layer: developmental stage.

3

HOW PLAY EVOLVES
WITH DEVELOPMENT

D
evelopmental stage is a very important aspect of your child's behavior and capabilities. Many behaviors parents think indicate a problem are actually completely natural for a child at the developmental stage they are in. Many of the things children can't do yet worry parents, too. *Shouldn't they be able to do X by now? How do they already know how to do Y?* Throughout this book, I'll often call out developmental stages because they are helpful in understanding why your child is doing certain things.

I could write a whole book about this, but let's keep it to play-relevant basics for right now. Here are the basic developmental stages you can expect for children from one to eight years old. These are averages, so don't worry if your child falls a little outside of these age ranges in any of the areas. It's likely nothing to worry about, but you can always talk to your pediatrician if you are concerned.

Age One

One-year-olds are taking first steps and honing their pincer grasp. Imagine that you are at the playground with your toddler. They begin to pick up tiny pieces of mulch and roll them between their fingers and bring them to their mouth. Your instinct might be to scold your little one and tell them that mulch is dirty, but your play-informed self knows they are working on an important skill. Of course, we don't want kids eating playground mulch! So, what can a parent do? Provide a small container and redirect them to pick up the mulch and put it in the container. Let them lead, and they'll likely become engaged in filling and dumping their container. This develops coordination and connection, and it sets a foundation for building play confidence.

One-year-olds are beginning to learn about cause and effect. When your baby continues to throw their cup off their high chair, remember that they want to know what will happen if they throw the cup. Rather than saying no, try verbalizing their developmental drive. "You are wondering where the cup goes when you throw it!"

This does two things. First, it removes the power struggle between caregiver and child. When adults have a big reaction, children will repeat the behavior because they need to have the adult react that way many times so that they can study and master the adult's large behavior. When the caregiver is calm and informed, even curious about the child's behavior, they can respond to the child instead of reacting. When your child throws the cup, and you respond by narrating, you can go deeper into the concept your child is working on: cause and effect.

But what about throwing that cup? You might let them throw it two or three times more, then say, "Bye-bye, cup!" and take away the cup. Then you can redirect them to other activities that reinforce the same lesson, like peekaboo, or providing toys that rattle or squeak.

One-year-olds are experiencing a strong attachment to care-givers, which can result in separation anxiety and parental prefer-ence. When your baby is crying for Dad, but Mom is giving the bath tonight, soothe them by saying, "You wish Dad was giving you a bath and tonight it is me. I know, you want Dad." Parents can hold a limit while also allowing their child to express their desires. Children tend to feel more comfortable with the parent they spend more time with or who meets their daily needs, although prefer-ences change over time as the child grows and their relationships with both parents continue to evolve. It will help everyone feel bet-ter if you try to remember that preferences are appropriate, tran-sitory, and not a sign of anything else.

Age Two

Twos are learning how to climb the stairs using handrails, they are running more than they walk, and many two-year-olds are just mastering how to kick a ball. They finally have the dexterity to turn the pages of a paper book as you read to them, and some might want to tear the pages. While we don't want to raise kids to deface property, we can recognize that their drive to exercise new-found fine motor skills is strong. Take away the book and replace it with a box top filled with scrap paper that they can tear up into tiny pieces. This will keep them busy for ages because you are pairing development with an appropriate task. Try letting them tear paper while you read to them.

Kids and stairs can be every parent's worst nightmare. It seems that the more you try to block the stairs, the more focused they are on wanting to climb up and down them! Take some time each day to allow them to practice going up and down the stairs holding on to the railing. They'll feel big and important as they carefully step up and down, and you'll feel great that they are working toward the milestone of being able to safely navigate the stairs. Walking up and down stairs as you sing or count is a great way to build skills and burn some energy before naptime.

Has your two-year-old's vocabulary started to explode? It is such an exciting time for parents. Think back to all that crying they did as newborns, when you desperately wished they could communicate their needs to you. It's all starting to happen now! As their language skills rapidly expand, you might see an uptick in tantrums and physical behavior. You can support your child by slowing things down and giving them time to process and think about what they want to say and do. Repeat back to them what they said to you. This helps them feel heard and understood, thus reducing unwanted behaviors.

Your two-year-old is developing an inner drive for autonomy, and you have the power to support that drive. Get in the habit of looking for small opportunities to give them control. Rather than chasing them around with a tissue to wipe their nose, bring them a mirror and a damp cloth or some wipes. Have them practice wiping your nose, then wiping their own nose in the mirror. What other areas can you give back some control? A tiny bit of autonomy can result in a lot more cooperation.

Age Three

Your three-year-old can probably balance on one foot, jump, use scissors, and manipulate small objects. Three-year-olds are notorious for using scissors to cut things they shouldn't (their hair, their clothing, the tablecloth, etc.). Get ahead of this by knowing that your three-year-old is getting ready to practice with scissors. Give them lots of things they *may* cut and be sure to call out the things that are off-limits.

During one of my first years as a head teacher in a small nursery school, I will never forget looking over during rest time to see two children who had snuck scissors onto their mats and were quietly cutting one another's bangs. I panicked! Thankfully, their parents were calm and understanding, and I kept my job. What did I learn from that? I learned that preschoolers need more opportunities to cut enticing materials (that are not human hair). Rather than take the scissors away, we had a class meeting about when and where scissors were allowed to be used.

Then, the real work began. I collected bits and bobs of shiny foil, neon string, soft and thick yarn, and various thicknesses of paper. We put everything in a large shallow bin and put out the scissors. There was no assignment. There were no dotted lines to cut and paste on. The goal was not to create a craft. The goal was for the children to develop confidence in their cutting skills and experience various ways to cut.

You can get ahead of the inevitable cutting of clothes and hair with your own cutting box at home. Grab an old shoebox and place some magazine pages, strips of construction paper, a little sheet of tinfoil, and some thin fabric inside. Put some sturdy child-sized scissors inside (make sure they actually work) and let your child go to town! They'll love practicing, and you'll save a trip to the hair salon. Keep the box in your kitchen, and they'll play while you get your own stuff done.

Threes are insatiably curious. "Why?" questions are common at this age. Threes are also figuring out spatial relationships and the meaning of words like under, over, and beside, or tomorrow and yesterday. Something I absolutely love about threes is watching them sort through these spatial relationships. You might notice your three-year-old squeeze themselves inside a cupboard, and delight that they are *inside* of something! You'll see them climbing atop things like the table or the slide at the playground to be *on top* of something.

One way to encourage this development is with a simple game. Grab a bin or a plastic tub. Put it in the center of the room. Let your child climb in and out, flip it over, climb on top, etc. Narrate what they are doing. Once they get the idea, they can play this independently using stuffed animals or with small figures and magnetic tiles.

Threes are learning cooperative play, pretend play, and to have a better understanding of emotions. Three-year-olds are interested in books that talk about emotions. When kids have a vocabulary to match how they're feeling inside, their behavior reflects it. This is also a wonderful way for adults to understand how it feels to be three.

Age Four

Four-year-olds are beginning to throw and catch things, hop up and down, draw representationally, and are developing the ability to execute very precise hand dexterity. Much like the three-year-olds who cut their hair when learning to use scissors, four-year-olds are likely to brand the walls or their books with their name. Fours are finally mastering how to write their name, and they will want to do it often! Give your four-year-old a special blank journal and writing utensil. Tell them you've noticed how they are working on writing and drawing, and that this notebook is a great place to put their important work. Give them lots of opportunities to make marks and draw in appropriate places, and your walls will stay clean.

In my home, I have a set of wooden unit blocks from my childhood. On one of the blocks, in green marker, in four-year-old handwriting, is my brother's name. As kids, we knew we were not permitted to draw or color on our blocks. But my brother had a newfound skill and he proudly signed one of the blocks. I am so glad my mom never made him wash it off because now my own children build and laugh at the story of how their uncle wrote his name on a block many years ago.

Fours are learning more complex imaginative play. You'll notice your four-year-old becoming more interested in sorting the differences between real and pretend, to make sense of the world around them. They may become more worried about monsters or want to understand whether monsters are real or make-believe. As your child grows and begins to differentiate these, watch their play closely. It can provide valuable insights into the topics and ideas they are trying to understand.

Fours are beginning to define their friendships more clearly. They can understand the basic rules of games and structured turn-taking. They are typically interested in learning more about the emotions of others.

Silliness is a trademark of being four! Being silly, while sometimes hilarious, can also be hard on parents. Where is the line between what's appropriate and what's not? Of course, that's up to you and your tolerance level, but there is one thing I recommend to parents of fours: Try examining their silliness through a developmental lens, and engage them in conversation, rather than outright correcting them. Try, "Saying 'poopy' makes your brother laugh so much. I can see that. You love to make others laugh, don't you? Let's think of more ways you can make your brother laugh besides saying poopy all the time."

Or, "Do the children at school laugh when you do that? At home, you can make us laugh by telling funny jokes and pretending things. I love to laugh with you." You can try making a list together of things that make children laugh, combining your four-year-old's new understanding of peers and their desire to write words. Sometimes, let's be honest, "poopy" is funny, and it's okay for you to laugh at something you think is funny. However, when their choice of funny jokes is inappropriate in a certain situation, you can encourage them to choose something else on the list you made together.

Age Five

Most five-year-olds stop napping and have high energy levels, requiring more physical activity and playtime. Their fine motor skills continue to improve, so give your five-year-old lots of opportunities to practice. Put an old sneaker in the back seat of the car and let them try tying and untying the laces while they're riding. It will keep them engaged and support their shoe-tying in a no-pressure, no-judgment way.

The vocabulary of fives expands rapidly, and sentence construction improves. You will likely notice better communication skills in general. They begin to solve problems and make decisions on their own, though they still need adult assistance. Fives have improved memory retention, with the ability to recall past events and understand the concept of time better (like yesterday, today, and tomorrow). Many start recognizing letters and numbers and might show interest in reading and counting. If you are looking for a way to connect with your five-year-old, play memory games. They love the challenge. It will keep them focused and engaged, and you'll both have fun.

Fives display increased independence, deeper friendship formation, the development of empathy, a better understanding of rules, and a more complex expression of feelings. Your five-year-old is rapidly maturing, and now is a great time to revisit their role in the household. Do their daily routines match their capabilities? Say to them, "I've noticed that you really seem to be growing up. I bet you can do more than feed the dog and set the table. Do you think you can start remembering to bring in the garbage cans after school? They're pretty heavy. Should we practice and see if you can do it yet? What other jobs do you think would be good for a five-year-old like you?" This will appeal to your five-year-old's desire for more independence and their need to seek praise and approval from the adults in their lives. When they are involved in deciding and choosing what chores they are now able to do, the chores will feel more enticing.

Age Six

Six-year-olds continue to refine both gross and fine motor skills. Most six-year-olds will have established whether they are left- or right-handed. If your six-year-old isn't already obsessed, try introducing LEGOs or other small building materials. These support your child's growing fine motor skills and appeal to their problem-solving capabilities.

Many six-year-olds are starting to read or are already reading, and their comprehension skills are improving. Basic math skills and understanding of numbers improve, and some may start to perform simple calculations. While still limited, their attention span and focus improve, along with problem-solving skills and logical thinking.

Six-year-olds are often very curious and ask many questions to understand their environment and experiences better. They love to show off their skills. Have them write some labels for things around the house that they are learning to read or write, and tape them up—for example, the word "chair" taped to a kitchen chair. If you have a book lover, create some blank books by stapling a few blank sheets of paper together and providing markers and pencils. They'll feel so big and confident writing and sharing their own books and drawings with friends and family.

Six-year-olds typically enjoy playing with peers and can cooperate better in group activities. They show an understanding of their own and others' emotions, and they can express feelings more accurately. They start to develop a sense of right and wrong, and they may seek approval from adults. There's an increase in empathy and concern for others.

You might notice your six-year-old becoming a stickler for the rules when they play with you, siblings, and friends. Get curious. Ask them about the rules, and let them elaborate. Then, start to introduce the concept of flexibility within the rules. Let them know that you know how important the rules are to them. You can acknowledge that it is hard for them when they don't win. Keep playing games and modeling good sportsmanship while also holding space for their development.

Age Seven

Physically, seven-year-olds are getting even better at writing, drawing, and sports. Now that your child can write and draw, you can start communicating with them in this way! Leave them notes, and ask them to write back. This builds connection while playing to their strengths. "Hi, Ryan, I loved watching you swim today. You looked like you were having so much fun. I wonder what you were thinking about in the pool today? Write back! Love, Mom."

Sevens are beginning to think more critically and logically, though thinking can still be very concrete. A longer attention span allows for better focus on tasks and activities. They are developing an even better memory and strategies for learning and problem-solving. Do you wish your seven-year-old's behavior would be more reliable in the grocery store or the restaurant? Lean on their growing math skills. Have them add up menu items or give them a budget, and challenge them to choose this week's cereal selections.

Friends start to become more important to seven-year-olds. They seek approval from friends. They are developing skills in resolving conflicts with peers, though they are still learning how to do this. Even though sevens seem very independent, don't be fooled—they still need lots of support and reassurance from adults. If they don't already, try allowing your seven-year-old the opportunity to order for themselves in a restaurant. Have them practice using a clear voice or pointing to what they'd like on the menu. They'll feel grown-up, and you'll be teaching them an important life skill. Now is a great time to support their growing sense of independence from the sidelines.

Age Eight

Eights love to create, and they are getting good at coming up with a plan and executing it. What can they build or make that matches their interests? Eight is a great age to teach your child basic sewing machine skills or how to use a power drill.

Eights are improving their academic skills, with the ability to grasp more abstract and complex concepts. They have increased attention span and focus, which supports learning and task completion. Reading and writing skills are more advanced, and they can engage with and understand a wider range of materials. Homework challenges tend to increase around eight. Rather than fighting with your child, empower them. Teach them how to mark their homework questions/challenges in the margin and support them in communicating with their teacher rather than just doing it for them.

Friendships become increasingly important, and there's a strong desire for social acceptance. Eights are developing a more complex self-image and awareness of how they are perceived by others. Many parents are surprised at how moody their eight-year-olds are. Rest assured, this is typical as their emotional sense of self is rapidly developing. Rather than chastise them for their moody behavior, show some empathy for what they might be feeling. A little bit of understanding can go a long way. You can set a limit on behavior while also showing you understand their internal challenges. It might sound like this: "Earlier, you shouted at me to leave your room. It got me thinking that you are getting older, and that you would probably like more privacy. Can you help me come up with some ways to give you more privacy without shouting at me? Let's figure this out together."

You don't have to become an expert at child development to

tune in to how your child is growing and changing. Noticing the skills they are attempting to master through their play and knowing that some of their struggles are completely normal for their age can help you to connect with them on a more empathetic level. You'll also get better at observation—the subject of the next chapter. Let this chapter and the one before it be a window into your child's personality and preferences to help you support their play and growth. Through careful observation, you can get an even clearer view.

OBSERVE YOUR CHILD
TO GUIDE THEIR PLAY

We all watch our kids, but intentional observation can reveal things about your child you might not have consciously noticed before. By taking the time to watch how your child plays, interacts with others, and approaches challenges, you may discover hidden talents, recurring behavioral patterns, or areas where they might benefit from additional support.

When observing children, pay attention to various aspects of their behavior and interactions. Nonverbal cues, such as body language and facial expressions, and how children react in different situations, can reveal a lot about a child's feelings and needs, especially before they can fully articulate them verbally. By considering these factors, parents can gain a deeper understanding into how their child's mind works and how to set them up for successful self-directed play.

Let's say you notice that your child talks about cats a lot, and always points out the stuffed cats in the toy store. Cats: check. But you can go deeper. What is it about cats that they love so much?

Do they love cats because they are interested in nurturing and caring for another living being? Is it that cats seem a little like wild animals, and they are fascinated by the freedom in acting wild? Is it that they are attracted to how cats communicate with body language, or their precise and careful movements? You can ask your child what they like, but you'll gain much more insight into the inner workings of their mind by *observing* them for a few moments each day. You can use the information you gathered to inform how you support your child's independent play.

What would that look like? It might mean planting some cat picture books around your home in a few key spots, and then watching your child discover them. Maybe it means putting a small stool by the window for your child to sit and watch for the neighborhood cat crossing your front yard, as it does each day. It could be as simple as putting a few cat figurines out on the table with a small lump of play dough and watching your child create. The idea is not that you want your child to become a cat expert; the idea is that you want to use your child's interests to further their drive to be curious, seek information, and execute ideas. Their interest in cats is what will draw them in, but their drive for knowledge, skill building, and autonomy is what will keep them playing.

Peeling back another layer of observing, consider those small moments that are part of your daily routine. Say your child is eating in their high chair. They are finally occupied, so you may be tempted to get something done. But wait—consider observing your child during these mundane moments. Whether they are in their high chair, car seat, or playing, what are they choosing to do when they aren't relying on you to occupy them? This isn't about interpreting your child's behavior. This is about training yourself to notice your child and the experience they are having on their own.

Get in the habit of observing your child when you are not inter-acting directly with them. Here are some things to tune in to:

- Listen to your child's self-talk for insights into their thought processes.

- Pay attention to transitions and frustrations. When your child gets frustrated, you may be tempted to jump in and smooth things over—instead, take a moment to see what your child does. See the box about "The Magic Pause" on the next page.

- Notice how different environments impact your child.

If your child becomes aware that you are watching them, or even if they don't, you can tell your child, "Your play is very inter-esting and important. One way that grown-ups learn more about things they are interested in is by watching. The grown-up word for that is called 'observing.' I want to learn more about how you play on your own, so you might notice me watching you and writ-ing things down. When I am observing, pretend I'm not even there. Pretend I am invisible, and you are doing important work. Do you have questions about that?"

Occasionally, share your observations with your child to help them become more aware of their own interests and skills. You can do this by narrating their play and neutrally describing what you see, rather than trying to influence it or express an opinion about it. They'll delight in the details you noticed about their play and likely will excitedly tell you *more* about their thinking. Re-member, the goal is not to judge or influence but to understand and support, creating an environment that encourages more fre-quent and sustained periods of independent play.

Keeping track of your observations over time can be enlighten-ing, but you may not be sure exactly how to do it. When observing

THE MAGIC PAUSE

When observing your child, or in that moment when you finally get to sit down for the first time in hours, you may hear that familiar refrain: "Mom, I need help!" (How do kids always seem to know the exact moment that you just sat down? Can they smell it?) Your first impulse might be to jump right up to help, but wait. Stop! First, check out this tip that might change how you respond.

"The Magic Pause" is one of the best-kept secrets when it comes to raising independent kids, but what is it? A Magic Pause is simply a way to give your child a moment to figure out how to do something on their own independently.

When your child calls you, pause. Count backward from ten in your head. Hold that space for ten seconds and give your child the opportunity to figure it out. They may surprise you and respond with, "Never mind, I got it," before you even finish counting to one.

When they figure it out on their own, try saying something like this: "That was hard, and you kept trying. It worked! You thought you needed help, but you figured it out!"

If pausing doesn't work for your child, they likely need some time to grow into it. Try five seconds, or even three. Help them build frustration tolerance by not rushing in to rescue. After pausing, go to your child and say: "Show me what you've tried so far." This kind of response communicates to them that it is okay to try on their own. If your child has a hard time waiting for you, try saying, "You wanted me to come right away, and I didn't. I am here now." Or, "It's hard to wait!"

The Magic Pause is the space that both you and your

child need in order to remember that your child is a capable human who is developing new skills and independence every day! Mastering The Magic Pause will take time! That is okay. Keep practicing!

children at play, here's the template I like to use. You can copy this or create one that makes the most sense for you:

Begin by writing down exactly what you see happening. That might look like this:

10:00—Tommy sits at the table. Reaches for play dough.
10:01—Squeezes play dough in both hands. Says "Squishy!"
10:02—Rolls play dough into a ball. Smashes ball with palm.
10:03—Picks up a plastic knife. Attempts to cut play dough.
10:04—Struggles with knife. Frowns. Says "Help, Mama."
10:05—I help him with hand placement. He tries again.
10:06—Successfully cuts play dough. Smiles widely.
10:07—Picks up cut pieces. Starts stacking them.
10:08—Stack falls. Tommy laughs. Says "Again!"
10:09—Begins rolling the play dough into a long "snake."
10:10—Coils "snake" into a spiral. Says "Snail!"

Then, record what you noticed. That might look like this:

• Tommy often likes to both build up and break apart the play dough.
• He's getting better at rolling and cutting compared to last week.
• He is using some new words.
• He likes stacking and smashing repeatedly.

Next, jot down any ideas for next time:

- Is he ready for a new tool, like a cookie cutter?
- Try giving him a mallet?
- How can I build on his work? Can we go to the library to find a book about snakes or snails?

When you pay attention to the small things and mention them later, it really shows kids you value their work, even if what they did seemed small or insignificant. This builds confidence in your child and the understanding that their play is important and that you actually care about it.

Are You Playing "For" Your Child?

When grown-ups practice observing their child's play, something very important happens. The grown-up becomes aware of how much they've previously been stepping in and intervening in their child's play. You may find you are tempted, or have to stop yourself, from commenting, fixing, or trying to teach your child something. Stay strong!

When children ask me to join their game, I almost always say no. I tell them the truth: "When grown-ups play in children's games, the magic disappears." It is very tricky for adults to play with children without accidentally taking over or influencing, but this is crucial for the child to learn how to play independently.

I call this playing *for* your child. When you do this, you take away the child's agency to play in their own way. This is why I emphasize observing rather than adding your input. This makes it about you, when the most important thing about play is that it's about your child and their world.

Let's recall the child who is interested in cats. You've observed them and you know they love cats. You put out a few cat figurines and a lump of play dough. They eagerly approach the table and reach for the dough. You lovingly say, "Look! You can make a house for your cats! Where do cats sleep? Can you create a cat bed? Here, let me show you how . . ."

Although you had the best of intentions, you just robbed your child of the opportunity to follow their own train of thought around cats. I want you to look at play as an opportunity for your child to pose their own questions and seek their own answers. It is the parents' job to support and nurture play, not create it. It is the child's job to create and develop their play ideas—even the American Academy of Pediatrics says so!

When children play without adult direction, they use their imagination more. So, what can you do instead? You already did the important part—you provided open-ended materials for your child to work out their thinking about an interest they have. Now you get to do what parents do best: sit back, watch your child, and admire this amazing being in front of you. Listen and watch without interjection. This may be difficult if you are in the habit of voicing your opinion about what your child should or could be doing while playing. Try not to keep saying "good job!" or "do it this way." This actually puts pressure on them. Their play turns into a bid for more praise, fear of doing it wrong, or a performance for you. If your child keeps asking you to participate or asks you questions, briefly answer them and redirect them back to what they are working on. It gets easier the more you practice.

Think about the last time you played with your child. Who was in charge? Whose ideas were expressed? Who led the play? In

WHAT ABOUT ONLY CHILDREN?

If you have an only child, do you feel more obligated to play with them than you would if they had siblings? Since I have three children, I decided to ask my colleague Stacy McAnn, licensed therapist and proud mom of one child, to get her perspective. Here's what she said:

When you have an only child, you do have to resign yourself to the fact that you are going to play with your child more than if that child had siblings. There is a level of acceptance about this that every parent of an only child will have to think about. That said, I still think it's vitally important to put boundaries around play and teach independent play skills as early as possible.

With only children, although you will engage your child more often as their only partner in the home, you do not want to be the default partner for everything they do. That's why it's even more important to work on independent play with an only child. This isn't easy for parents to navigate because there is a societal judgment that makes them feel guilty for not giving their child any siblings. That judgment leads to the feeling that you can't expect your child to play alone. Many parents can't even wrap their head around the idea that their only child could play independently.

So how do you give your only child the chance to develop a sense of autonomy and creativity? Instead of thinking in terms of playing with your child, think in terms of engaging with your child. Ultimately, that's a positive thing about having an only child. You form a very tight-knit family unit because you're engaging more often. That doesn't mean playing.

There is a significant difference between playing with

your child and engaging with your child. Just as the parent needn't be the default playmate, play needn't be the default method for connection. As an adult person and mother, I have a lot of things on my mind. To have the mental and emotional capacity to be at my best for my kid, I can't always be sitting on the floor playing princess. I can't even do it at all most of the time. That's why engaging your child in other types of activities is supportive of your own mental health as a mother.

We want other activities to be just as valuable and wanted by the child, but to the child, they may still be play. Play to a child is not just toys, pretend, baby dolls, and trucks. Play for children, especially under six, happens in a wide variety of contexts.

Expand how you think about play. Baking muffins is play for my three-year-old. Putting together the IKEA shelf is play for a four-year-old. Expanding the definition to include things that we need or would like to do anyway helps us alleviate some of the guilt we might feel when we're not playing in the traditional sense. When you can engage in a better way, you will be at your best with them. It's a gift you give yourself. If I can make muffins with my child instead of playing on the floor, I'm going to be way better for her in three hours when we go to the library. And when she plays on the floor by herself, she'll get to exercise her own ideas.

Whatever you do, if your number one priority is attuning to your child's needs and engaging or connecting to them in some way, then you're doing fine. You don't need to have siblings to benefit from that attunement and that deep relationship. Play, engagement, connection, and especially teaching the skill of independent play will get you far.

many cases, parents are surprised to recognize it was them, not their child.

Before you start feeling like you're failing at yet another aspect of parenting, know this: You aren't doing anything wrong. Your child likely loves it when you play for them! You are connecting with your child in a positive way, and I will never tell you to stop doing that. However, since you are reading this book because you want your child to learn to play independently, it is my job to show you that play is their work, not ours. Our role is to support them, not play for them.

One of my first years teaching fours, I had an assistant whom the children adored. They were exuberant, warm, kind, funny, and inclusive of all of the children in our classroom. They knew just how to make them laugh and the silliest songs to sing, and they made the best voices when reading to the class. What a gem.

But . . . there was something that was bothering me. I found myself becoming increasingly frustrated in the classroom and I could not figure out why. Was I jealous of their closeness with the children and their families? Did I wish I was better at making silly voices? After a lot of introspection, I came to understand that what was bothering me was that they were entertaining the children and playing for them, rather than allowing the children to do their most important work: figuring out how to play. (To be fair, this phenomenal person was new to teaching and went on to become a seasoned professional.)

I share this story to highlight that your role as a supporter of independent, self-directed play is to step out of the circus ring. Remove yourself from the role of entertainer and instead join the audience. You're in for a really good show.

I think a lot of parents, especially those who work out of the home, feel that when they are with their child, they should be interacting with them. Let's reframe what "interacting" means. It doesn't have to mean being the director. It can mean being an active listener and observer. It doesn't have to mean that you're opening your mouth and changing the path of their play. Interacting with them can be an engaged facial expression and body language.

Try adjusting how you interact with your child, from "What does the cow say" and "Put this piece over there," to sitting close and watching closely without making any noise. Or, only reflect what they're saying instead of saying your own thing. Your child's play will begin to look different in the most amazing ways.

Let's say you cherish bath time with your little one and often use it as a chance to play and connect. Here are two scenarios for how to connect during bath time. Both are examples of a loving exchange between parent and child. However, notice the difference in terms of supporting independent play:

Example 1: Parent-Directed Play

It's bath time, and you're excited to use this moment to teach your little one. As soon as they're in the tub, you say: "Let's play with letters! Can you find the blue A?" They hand you a foam letter. "Great job! Now, let's count the duckies. One, two . . ." You line up the rubber ducks. "Can you squirt water on the red duck?" You guide their hand to the water toy. You're having fun, but you're also running the show, deciding what to play and how.

Example 2: Supporting Self-Directed Play

It's bath time, and you're curious to see what your child will do. As they get in the tub, you sit close, leaning in with an attentive smile, but you don't say anything yet. Your little one picks up a cup, fills it with water, and pours it out. You simply narrate: "You're filling the cup . . . now you're pouring it out!" They grab a rubber duck and make it dive. You comment, "Oh, your duck is swimming!" When they splash excitedly, you laugh along: "Wow, big splashes!" You're fully engaged, but you're following their lead, showing interest in what they choose to do. You're learning about what captivates them while they drive their own play.

Again, this is a hard adjustment to make if you are in the habit of intervening, but you might be surprised that your child's motivation or purpose in their play is completely different than you thought it was.

Recently, I found a video of my daughter with a cup of grapes. She was about eighteen months old. She sat at the table, saying, "One, two, one, two . . ." as she moved the grapes. My first instinct was to correct her counting from "one, two, one" to "one, two, three." But, I resisted the urge. Instead, I simply watched and nodded, allowing her to complete her own process.

Eventually, she exclaimed, "I did it!" showing me the empty bowl with so much pride. That's when I realized she wasn't trying to count—she was exploring the concepts of empty and full. By resisting the impulse to correct her, I avoided derailing her self-chosen task and discovered her true interest.

I acknowledged her achievement, echoing her excitement: "You did do it! You emptied that bowl." This reinforced her sense of accomplishment and built her confidence in her ability to complete goals she set for herself. Understanding her interest in emptying and filling, I could now extend her play and support her exploration. Later that day, she sat at the sensory table with a bowl of water and two scoops and continued to experiment with empty and full. This experience reminded me to trust in my child's natural development.

The last thing I want to emphasize about observing your child is that ultimately, even though I'm suggesting you let your child lead, the truth is that you are actually leading—you are leading by letting them lead. You know your child best. You understand your child best. You are the expert on your child. Have confidence in your own knowledge of and intuition about your child. Never stop taking those opportunities for observation because as your child grows and develops, their interests will continue to change and there will constantly be new things to learn about them.

5

UNDERSTANDING THE CULTURE OF YOUR FAMILY

f I were to write you a play prescription for your children, telling you exactly what to say, exactly how to set up specific play areas, and exactly how your child should play, it probably wouldn't work. Even if you adapted everything I said in order to teach your child to play independently according to how I did it in *my* home, it would likely not yield hours of productive play in *your* home. Because your family culture is specific, the strategies I give you in this book must be adapted to fit the culture of *your* family.

Each family has their own priorities, values, and traditions, which come from their own culture, where they live and have lived, who their friends are, how they were raised, and what they have decided is most important in life. A family's culture influences how your family interacts, how your household works, how your schedules and environment affect what you are all able to do—and how your children play.

Here are some examples: Does your family love to gather around the football game and bond over competitive sports? Or maybe your family loves art and books, and your weekends are centered around reading, painting, or visiting the library and the local museum. Are you a traveling family who values learning about other places? Or you might be the house on the block that prefers a quieter, more private lifestyle. Do your kids tend to gather together in one room most of the time, or do they prefer individual spaces to decompress? Maybe a home-cooked family dinner at the table is sacred in your house, or just the opposite—everyone grabs food and eats at their convenience, and you come together in different situations, like for traveling, or when everyone attends someone's game or performance.

Honoring your family's unique rhythms in play and parenting is crucial for fostering a playful home environment. Forcing unnatural parenting styles or activities can lead to inconsistency and parental burnout, negatively impacting both parents and children. This is confusing for kids because they don't know what to expect or which version of you they will get. Instead, focus on what feels genuine and sustainable for your family. By embracing your family's natural patterns rather than adhering to external "shoulds," you create a more consistent, enjoyable, and effective parenting experience.

So, with your own family's culture in mind, let's get your children playing in a way that feels authentic and sustainable to you. For example, my best friend's son loves hockey. They are a family of hockey fans, and this is how they bond. She told me, "He can't have quiet time. He can't play independently—all he wants to do is talk about hockey. He wants to watch the highlights, talk about stats, and get outside and play hockey with friends! I know he needs downtime, but it's not working."

I knew how much the boy needed quiet time, and as a close friend of the family, I also knew how integral it was for Mom to have some downtime as well. She had a newborn at home, and there was an older sibling in the picture, too. Dad was busy at work, and Mom didn't have a lot of support at home. She was a playful, creative mama, but she was losing that side as she ran herself ragged with three kids and no break.

When thinking about self-directed play and kids, I always suggest taking a strengths-based approach. I knew this four-year-old was active and competitive and needed an outlet for his brilliant mind. He was (and still is) great at hockey, and he felt confident in his knowledge on the subject. So we started there. How could we bring in his love of hockey and make it appropriate for quiet play?

Here's what we did: We put his toy hockey guys on a table. We added markers and a large sheet of paper. On one of the sheets of paper we drew a simple hockey rink and put his guys nearby. Then we stood back to see what would happen. After some moments of resistance, her son became really invested in playing *about* hockey during his daily quiet time. He began to invent hockey plays, drawing them out, then enacting them with his hockey guys. He loved to watch hockey games and stats on TV, and then re-create that day's plays he had watched. His mom had always tried to limit his TV time, but each new thing he watched gave him ideas and motivation to invent and strategize, creating more hockey scenarios. He used to have a difficult time when the TV went off, but now he began to get excited about how to play based on what he had watched. We started him with the hockey drawing, but it ended up expanding. He began to use many open-ended materials for his hockey play. He would make a hockey rink out of blocks and play with the guys in there. Sometimes he would use play dough or draw more detailed rink setups and play ideas. His mother told me she felt really good about giving him an outlet to explore his interests beyond just watching TV and playing with his team. He used to want her to watch him play hockey or play hockey with him, but now he had a satisfying outlet to play on his own. Understanding your family culture can also help you to curate your family activities. Rather than signing up for everything (or nothing), you can prioritize activities that are in line with your family values. Let's look at how you can begin to define and refine your family culture by beginning with your values.

Defining Your Family Values

Knowing your values can help you create a rhythm for your family that meets everyone's needs. It can reduce stress and minimize guilt. I know that when I feel parental guilt, it's usually because I'm misaligned with my values. Maybe I'm rushed, and I'll do something for my kids that I know they should have done for themselves. Then I get annoyed with myself and them. Sometimes it can seem like life is so hectic, we just do what we can to get through the day . . . then we lie awake at night thinking about what we should have done. Then in the morning we just press PLAY and do it all again.

This kind of dynamic can create an uneasy feeling you may not be able to define, but it is often because your behavior is conflicting with your values or beliefs. This is common with mothers who want to be one kind of parent but find themselves acting in misaligned ways because of stress and overwhelm. This is why alignment with your values is so critical for a peaceful family environment—but first you have to stop and take a little time to determine what your family values actually are.

Just to be clear, you will never 100 percent solve this problem. There will always be some sort of misalignment, but you can find a more comfortable balance most of the time. Consciously understanding your family values can help to calm the noise and reduce the pressure. We all thrive off rest and play. Imagine looking forward to a weekend that is full of activities you all love to do (rather than obligations you dread). One family might be excited to plan an elaborate family hike on the weekend, while another family would much prefer to stay home and have a break from the busy week. Understanding what kind of family you are can help you decide which activities to do and which to pass on.

You can start thinking about your core family values right now. Begin by assessing what feels aligned in your life and what feels misaligned. Answer these questions on your own, with your partner, or even include the kids:

- Are you as busy as you want to be or too busy?
- Are your kids doing activities they don't really love and you don't love attending?
- Is there too much socializing or not enough?

Next, start thinking about your family "vibe"—what descriptive word or words best describe your family? And is that the way you *want* to be? Your vibe may be one thing now, but it can change, and *you* get to be the one to change it. Remember: You don't need to stick to one category. Many families have diverse and wide-ranging interests. However, narrowing down what really matters to you and scheduling your family accordingly can make your life feel more centered and fulfilling.

Accepting	Grateful	Political
Adaptive	Hardworking	Private
Adventurous	Homebodies	Productive
Artistic	Honest	Reliable
Bookish	Intellectual	Religious
Calm	Inventive	Reserved
Casual	Jokesters	Respectful
Cohesive	Kind	Responsible
Communicative	Leaders	Safe
Creative	Listeners	Secretive
Cultured	Motivated	Sentimental
Disciplined	Musical	Social
Dramatic	Nature-Loving	Sophisticated
Dreamers	Nurturing	Spirited
Energetic	Old-Fashioned	Spiritual
Entrepreneurs	Opinionated	Sporty
Faithful	Orderly	Travelers
Frugal	Passionate	
Generous	Performers	

Add any other words that describe your ideal family vibe:

_____

_____

_____

Do the things you *do* every day align with the vibe described above? If not, how can you change that? It's easy to let the day-to-day minutiae get in the way of the larger values you want to uphold. But you *can* make space to do the things you need to do while also keeping the umbrella of what is important to your family in the forefront.

What do you all love doing together? Going to the movies, going on day trips, and now you never have time for it? This is about being intentional about how your family spends their time, not just letting life happen to you.

For example, if you chose "travelers," "cultured," and "adventurous," but you sign your children up for two sports per season and say yes to every school function and volunteer opportunity invitation that comes your way, then your family life probably feels overextended and misaligned. There is absolutely nothing wrong with signing up for all the sports teams, the PTA, and lots of social events! That's fantastic if your family values are in line with "sporty," "spirited," and "social." But if you're aiming for a more spontaneous family life of impromptu weekend museum visits or out-of-town trips, you're setting yourself up for failure by keeping your weekends so busy. Your values aren't aligned with your actions.

Here's another controversial example: birthday parties. You don't have to go to every child's birthday you are invited to; it's okay to say no. If you value family time or downtime on weekends, you are allowed to protect that time and politely decline an invite. This is an aha moment for many moms! But doing what's best for your family—even at the risk of going against the norm—is how you respect your family culture. It doesn't matter what other families do. I'll be honest: I've gotten a lot of blowback on this particular opinion (birthday parties are a sacred rite in many communities!), but I stand by my stance putting your child's mental health and well-being before all else. If you're dragging your kids to every birthday party and they are having meltdowns, you don't have to do that. As a parent, you know what your children need.

When my children were small—ages six, four, and one—we spent our entire weekends going from peewee soccer to T-ball, while squeezing in a birthday party after naps, then heading to a block party in the late afternoon. My husband and I had signed the kids up for soccer and T-ball because that's what everyone else was doing, so it felt natural and "correct." It was also exhausting.

I was a stay-at-home mom, and my husband worked long, intense hours. I solo-parented all week long and yearned for a little relaxation on the weekends—and yet, we would power through with little or no downtime. The truth was, my son never really liked soccer. He spent more time staring up at the airplanes and imagining their flight patterns than he did playing the actual game. My daughter liked T-ball, but she also really needed downtime to create and rest. My youngest daughter was still a tiny baby, just living life, attached to me in the baby carrier.

My husband and I loved to go out on the weekends with our friends, no kids, but I was literally too exhausted to even think about putting on a cute outfit and getting a babysitter. I was falling asleep when I tucked the kids in. We were doing too much, and our family life was not aligned with who we wanted to be or how we wanted to feel. I clearly remember asking my six-year-old son, "How do you really feel about soccer? Don't tell me yet! Think about it. If soccer feels really good to you and you have fun at practice and you like the games, we can keep doing it next year. If you just kind of like it, but you wish you were reading airplane books and playing in the backyard, if you don't feel excited about soccer, we aren't going to sign up next time."

Your child's opinion matters. I suggest asking your kids:

- "What's your favorite part of [this activity]? Take a moment to really think about it."

- "Imagine it's [activity] day. How does your tummy feel when you wake up? Do you have excited butterflies or nervous knots?"

- "If you could choose between [activity] and [activity], which would make you smile more? It's okay to be honest."

- "When you're doing [the activity], do you feel relaxed, or do you wish you were doing something else?"

- "Let's pretend there's no [activity] next week. Would you feel sad, relieved, or would you not mind either way? There is no right or wrong answer."

These are the kinds of questions you can ask your kids, to find out whether their activities are in line with *their* values and interests, or if they are just going along because you signed them up or because that's what all their classmates are doing. In our case, my son didn't really care that much about soccer, so we cut back on that and more. We began to honor our core family values, only attending birthday parties of close friends. We carved out weekend mornings to wander in the woods. I remember canceling one of the ballet activities, then telling my daughter, "We don't have to go to ballet anymore. Do you want to take the train into the city and play on the playground?" She was so excited; she couldn't believe we were able to do that.

There are also some questions you can ask yourself:

- "In what ways do our chosen activities support my child's growth and interests? Are there any we could add or remove to better serve these goals?"

- "How well does our schedule accommodate both the need for enrichment and the need for downtime?"

- "How can we creatively carve out quality family time within our busy schedules?"

- "For my child, what kind of environment helps them thrive? Do they need more structure or more free play? How can we fit that into a way that works for all of us?"

- "When I look at our family calendar, does it reflect a sustainable rhythm for all of us? Are there ways we can adjust to better support everyone's needs—parents and children?"

It was hard sometimes, and I second-guessed our choices more than once. It's never easy to do things differently than everyone else. Sometimes we were flexible and went to more than one party on a weekend. The difference was that it was intentional, not automatic. There were seasons (and still are) during which we feel more stressed with activities and commitments, but there are also seasons that feel slower, more relaxing, and more centering for the family. Keep your eye on what matters, and reserve the right to pull back when you need to.

You don't have to change everything at once, but as you gain insight into what truly matters to your family, you can gradually make choices that align with your values, fostering an environment where everyone can thrive. Remember that the key to success is taking action on the knowledge you have gained. With dedication and commitment, you can achieve the results you and your family deserve, and life is going to feel a lot lighter.

Consciously and intentionally defining your family values will bring them into the forefront of your thinking and parenting. You can lean on them when you are unsure, or when you or your child is struggling. You can call them to mind when you aren't sure how to handle a situation, or when you are assessing your family's obligations and activities.

This is so valuable for keeping you motivated and directed as

WHAT ABOUT CAREGIVERS?

If you struggle with how to manage your independent play values when your kids spend time with grandparents, other family members, or babysitters, you are not alone. If you were to peek inside my direct messages on Instagram, you'd likely see some version of the following question: "We've worked hard to establish an independent play routine for our kids, but when my mother-in-law watches them, they get so much screen time and she plays with them nonstop. They come home whining for more screens and it's like they forgot how to play independently. What should I do?"

It can feel frustrating to work so hard and feel like it's all been undone. I know I have felt that way when my kids were small. When someone else is offering to care for your child free of charge, you usually can't dictate how they spend their time. Most grandparents take pride and joy in playing with their grandchildren and giving them extras like screens and sweets. If it's once in a while, try to allow them grace in doing so.

When your child returns home, expect that there will be pushback on your play and screen routines. Expecting it will help you feel less thrown off-balance about it. Try saying to your children, "Things are different at Mammy and Pop's house than they are at our house. At their house, you are allowed to watch shows while you eat breakfast! How special. At our house, we watch our shows after naps. That's different. Mammy and Pops play with you. That must be exciting. It's different from how things are with Dad and me. At our house, you're learning to play on your own."

you begin to institute a new routine of independent play in your family. Knowing what your values are will help you gain more confidence in your parenting. Just remember to stay flexible. As families grow and change, their values may shift as well. Different family members may also have different values, as each child begins to establish their own beliefs and values, which they will discover through your family culture and also through independent play.

You might want to revisit this chapter every year or two, in case your family values need an update. A family with toddlers and preschoolers likely values different things than a family with grade-schoolers and tweens. However, at the heart, most of what really matters to you as a parent and as a person will likely stay pretty much the same, and it's great to know consciously what those values are.

6

PLAY GIVES
YOUR CHILD PURPOSE

ndependent play is more than something that improves the family dynamic and creativity. It does all that and more, but its most important role is how it benefits your child. In that way, play is a child's work. Play helps children to make sense of the world and who they are in the world. Independent play gives them purpose and develops their sense of autonomy and individuality. It is essential for healthy early childhood development.

This doesn't just happen in humans. We've all seen those adorable videos of bear cubs tackling one another in the woods or puppies tangled together with their littermates as they nip, yelp, and roll around. More than just cute, play serves as an important skill builder for baby animals and humans alike. Puppies engage in play with littermates to hone important skills like motor coordination, feeding order, and social learning. Those are all things that will help them survive and thrive in the world. Similarly, play in early childhood allows children to practice living in the world.

Giving your child the opportunity to play will impact their

physical, social, emotional, cognitive, and language development. Creating opportunities for your child to play will lead them on a path of self-discovery where they'll relieve stress, make their own choices, and process the world around them. It's easy to think about play as something reserved for the ball field or the playground, but I want to challenge you to look outside of the obvious reasons play is great for your child. When you choose to look more closely at your child's play, you'll see that the skills they are gaining will impact them well past the playroom. Play gives your child purpose.

A Child's Purpose

For most adults, a sense of purpose gives us a reason to get up in the morning. It might be taking care of our children, working on a health or wellness goal, or seeking a promotion at our jobs. For kids, a sense of purpose is different. Children live in a world where the grown-ups tell them what to do and when to do it. Their lives are orchestrated from the time they wake up until they lay their heads down at night. In play, children have the opportunity to hold the baton.

If your child isn't connecting to their sense of purpose through play, this chapter will help you make small changes to support them in getting there. You won't always be able to make sense of their play, but you can rest assured that their play is giving them exactly what they need: a sense of agency in their own world.

The other day, I asked my daughter if she wanted to tag along with me to go to the supermarket. As the youngest of three, she usually jumps at any opportunity for alone time with Mom. To my surprise, she said, "I can't. I just got such a good idea about something I want to play with my magnetic tiles." My husband and I exchanged looks over her head as she marched off into her room.

"She uses those tiles nonstop," he said. Within minutes, we heard the sounds of clicking magnetic tiles coming from her room. It's empowering for kids to have their own idea and follow it through. Instead of going with the flow of coming along with Mom, she used her own idea and her materials to pursue a purpose we didn't need to understand.

Also notice how she was enacting her ideas with materials she plays with frequently. This is important. New toys and materials, and the sense of novelty they give children, is fun. But the benefit of working with the same toys and materials over and over is that kids don't need to start to think about how to use them. They already understand. Their hands and minds just know what to do, for whatever story they are trying to tell and problem they are trying to solve. Like an artist can pick up a paintbrush and start working, rather than having to figure out how the paint works and spreads, repeating play with the same materials allows your child to become adept at it and play out whatever they are working on, at a deeper level.

As a preschool teacher, I often allowed the children to leave up the things they built for multiple days in a row, and I was sure to offer the same art materials repeatedly. This gave the children the opportunity to anticipate how they wanted to use the materials and gave them the option to continue working through an idea from the day prior. It allowed them to become familiar with the materials so that their ideas could take center stage.

I consulted for a preschool that was introducing a new collage project each day for "collage week." They wanted to teach collage techniques, which is fine, but instead of giving the children an entirely new collage project with completely different materials each day, I advised them to put out the same materials each day so the children could master how to use the materials and use the glue. Kids need to master the mechanics of how something works before they can freely progress to getting more creative and innovative. I assured them that if they allowed the children to master the materials without changing them each day, the first few collages might be rudimentary, but by Friday, they would see some fantastic things they would never see if the children had to start from square one every day. Rather than copying what the teacher is doing, the children would be free to develop their own ideas.

The best thing about collage is that it gives kids the opportunity to sort and organize materials in ways that make sense to them, while they are also learning other skills like how glue works and how to manipulate and attach materials to paper. Have you seen those sites where you can "Download 200 ideas for your kids to do over winter break!"? This is exactly the opposite of what helps kids go deep. We want kids to master the materials first, and then they can use them in their own way rather than getting stuck in the preliminary stage of learning the mechanics. You can either learn a million things a little bit, or you can learn a few things and really dive into something and figure out what's important to you, building self-confidence and skills beyond the basics.

Maybe you've done this—offering new craft projects and toys each day, thinking that the novelty will draw the child into play and keep them from getting bored. But when we do that, we might take away the chance for the child to complete a project or develop and refine what they are trying to figure out. We rob them of their purpose. When they start a new type of play each day, they have to start over each day. It is beneficial to pull out the same set of blocks from yesterday or the same pile of LEGOs that they've been tinkering with. You don't have to reinvent the wheel every single day.

Independent play will look different for each child, especially when you've allowed your child to take the reins. What they do might not look like anything groundbreaking to you. Trust in your child. They might sift through the recycling and patch items together with a roll of masking tape to create a home for a worm they found on the walk home from school. They might build a LEGO airplane or line up colored blocks until they look just right to them. Your child might not be practicing math facts or memorizing sight words, but when you look more closely, you may see that they are working with skills they will need in school in a way that's more meaningful. The home for worms helps them understand balance and volume. The LEGO airplane helps them understand counting and basic physics principles. When they are drawing and creating, they are actually learning about learning, not by doing what someone else says, but by approaching learning in a way that is more internally motivated by them.

They've likely spent much of their day focusing on things that matter to others—their teachers, classmates, and parents. Play gives them the opportunity to look inward and focus on working with, building, creating, or acting out what matters to them. Make no mistake—they are learning. We know through research that learning outcomes achieved through play are better integrated.

You don't have to be creative or put a lot of thought into providing these experiences. You don't have to take much time or even buy anything. There are so many ways you can easily facilitate this. One day I was picking up my youngest from her grandparents' house, and I noticed a jar of random nuts, bolts, and heavy screws on my father-in-law's workbench. I asked him if I could take the jar. I had an idea. He laughed knowingly and handed over the jar.

When we got home, I took out a baking sheet and dumped the contents of the jar so that they spread evenly across the surface. I left them out on the kitchen counter next to a stack of cookies and a glass of milk. When my son came home from first grade that day, he beelined for the cookies and then became immersed in the tray of parts. There was nothing to "build," and no set of instructions. He could do whatever he wanted with them.

I didn't verbally call my son's attention to the tray of parts, and I didn't direct him or tell him what I thought he should do with them. I didn't even say, "Look what I found at Grandpa's house! I thought you might like to play with those." Instead, I let him discover, decide, and act on his own. When you want your child to invest in their play, allowing them to discover their own purpose is so important. I'll say this often throughout this book: Don't intervene in your child's play. You can set the stage and watch the show, but you are not a writer, producer, or performer.

We kept that jar on a shelf for years, and from time to time, I would pull it down and leave it out for play. Over the years, all three of my kids spent hours arranging the parts, putting them together in different ways, and taking them apart again. They liked the heaviness in their hands and the opportunities for play that the parts provided.

As my son grew older, his competence with tools grew. He learned that he loved the satisfaction it brought him to take things apart and put them back together another way. He began tinkering with bicycles, merging his passion for speed and precision. In fifth grade, he began to give bike lessons in the neighborhood and to tune up bikes in our garage for money. When he turned fourteen, he got his first real job at our town's bike shop. I can't prove this all began with that cookie sheet of parts, but I can't prove it didn't.

Observe and Support

The first step to supporting your child's play is to observe. In chapter 4, I talked about how to begin observing your child's play to learn more about who they are. You can also use your observations to gain a better understanding of what drives your child's play. As you observe, you will gain a deeper grasp on what motivates them, interests them, and what developmental needs they may be grappling with. Knowing those things will not only help you support their play, but it will also help you parent from a place of connection and understanding.

Let's take the example of my son who loved to tinker and build and compare him with my daughter, who was more drawn to art and design. While my son would use the nuts and bolts to figure out how to put them together, she would take the same tray of parts and line them up in various patterns and shapes. My youngest, who is a creator of stories and songs, would take those parts and set up an imaginary game where she would be selling the various items in a store or using them as food for her stuffed animals.

Why does this matter? They all played with the same jar of nuts and bolts, yet they were all different ages and at different developmental stages, and they each had different purposes for playing the way they did, based on who they are as individuals. While you don't need to understand the *purpose* behind your child's play, paying attention to *what* your child is doing can give you a deeper glimpse into their development as a person. Noticing the nuances in your child's play allows you to appreciate just how profound play is in your child's life. Understanding that your child's play has a purpose can motivate you to create an environment and a lifestyle that supports rather than dictates the unique path of their growth.

WHY KIDS MIGHT BUILD FORTS

Have you ever noticed that your child is drawn to small, enclosed spaces like forts and secret hideaways? Maybe you've been at the playground and looked up and frantically noticed your child was nowhere to be seen, when you hear their little voice calling, "Mama! Look at me. I'm in here!" And they've tucked their body into the small open cube on the climber.

Have you ever been at a preschool where a crying child sits inside their personal cubby, enveloping themselves with the familiar smell of home as they tuck their damp cheeks into their jacket or blankie for comfort?

Small spaces can offer a sense of security to children, especially when the world feels big or overwhelming. This is one of the reasons why they love to build forts. You may not like it when your child pulls out all the kitchen chairs and sheets and blankets from the linen closet to build their own fort—or at least you dread having to put everything back again—but here's why this activity is so attractive to children.

Even at home, a small space can provide comfort. Creating that space yourself can provide a sense of control. Many families have the very popular play couches that can be manipulated to create a fort or enclosure. These are so trendy right now because they make it easy for kids to create their own private space.

When I was a child and the world felt chaotic (I'm one of five kids, so there was always chaos), I would shut myself in the bathroom and climb into the empty bathtub to read. When my daughter was small, I pulled the end of her bed away from the wall and tacked up a blanket so she could make herself a space for when she was feeling overstimulated. She often sat in there with a flashlight, a book, and her favorite blankie. Small spaces can give children a feeling of autonomy and support sensory regulation. Think about how you can support this.

Once you learn to see your child's play as purposeful, you can't unsee it. A switch will flip in your brain, and you won't want to turn it off. When you understand more clearly why your child's play is so important for them individually, you'll find yourself saying yes to more of your child's ideas, even if they temporarily dismantle the living room, like fort building.

Reinforcing Your Child's Play Purpose

As you see your child progressing toward or achieving mastery over certain skills, you can use your observations to support, encourage, and affirm your child after the play is over. Build in ways to reflect on the work they are doing. At dinnertime or bedtime, you might tell your child something you noticed that they were working on, in a supportive and affirmative way. Leave room for curiosity. This will help your child feel seen and appreciated for their work.

Here are just a few examples of open-ended observations you can make to your child about their play, after the play is over, to help them feel seen. These are just to get you started—tailor these in whatever way is authentic to you:

- "Last week you were building zigzag tracks for your trains, and this week they are longer with winding curves. I wonder what was happening when the train zipped by?"

- "You were selling Silly Strawberry Smoothies all afternoon! What ingredients were in there? Your customers looked very happy!"

- "It used to be so tricky for you to balance on your scooter, and today I saw you zooming up and down the driveway."

Be intentional about using neutral language. "Good job on your scooter today!" closes the conversation. The point was to praise your child. More neutral, open-ended comments simply express what you saw. Then they have the opportunity to tell you about their experience, whether they were proud of what they did or wished they could have done something differently. You might even discover that their purpose was not at all what you thought.

After you comment, wait and let them choose to respond, or not. The point is not to solicit an answer—this is not meant to be a play interrogation! This is only to let them know you noticed and appreciated what they were doing, discovering, and developing as they played. The overall goal is for them to know their play is valued. If they choose to tell you more, great! If not? That is perfectly okay, too.

The most important thing to remember is to stay curious and open as you begin to look for your child's purpose in their play. As they play, they are reworking life experiences so that they make sense, developing problem-solving skills, and following their own pace. As you learn more from them and discover how incredibly enriching play experiences are for your child's overall growth and development, you'll find yourself prioritizing their play and happily (and knowingly) standing back to watch but not participate.

7

DECODING
YOUR CHILD'S PLAY

t may not always be obvious exactly what purpose a child is getting out of play, and I want to emphasize that you don't *have to
understand* the purpose of your child's play. You can simply sit
back and trust that their play has a meaning. However, if you start
paying attention to what your child is doing and the way they
are doing it, you will likely begin to see some recurring themes
emerging.

Think about your child's favorite things to do and ask yourself,
why do they always want to play the Paw Patrol game, or why are
they so often drawn to the dollhouse or the Spider-Man costume?
Let's look at some ways children often play and think about what
the purpose might be behind the play.

Block Play

In play, kids create a world where their choices matter. They can learn through their mistakes, choose revisions, experiment, and more. Think about your child creating a block building. Even a simple tower involves a large number of decisions, like choosing which block to start with, how to use hands for block placement, and whether the goal is height or the impact the tower will make when crashing down. Decision-making skills lay the foundation for intelligent choices and problem-solving capabilities in the future. Nurturing decision-making skills early helps them get confident at making decisions.

Block play has other potential purposes. When your child repeatedly builds towers and knocks them down, they are developing hand strength and dexterity. They're challenging their growing sense of cause and effect, and perhaps most importantly, experiencing the glee that is control over their environment.

Watch them, trust them, and provide space and time to do more of it. Are you never supposed to build with them? Of course not. Play can be a fun way to connect with your child. Just be sure they have plenty of time to play with those blocks without your help, guidance, or intervention.

Doll Play

I had a client with a newborn baby and two-and-a-half-year-old son who was adjusting to his new sibling. She told me how her toddler received a baby doll from his aunt, and she described how sweet he was when taking care of his new baby. She observed him as he rocked the doll in his arms and got a stool to climb on so he could gently place the doll in his sister's crib for sleepy time. She thought it was so cute!

Her toddler was using doll play to process his new way of life. I encouraged this mother to observe her toddler at play for more clues into his adjustment to being a brother. Over time, I worked with them to set up a baby area for her toddler. We added a preemie diaper and some wipes, a small doll stroller, and a box the child pretended was a crib for his doll. This gave the child the ability to play about what he was learning and process the big changes in his home environment.

One day, her toddler was yelling at the doll to stop crying and go to sleep! This gave Mom the opportunity to bond with her child by saying, "Yeah, babies sure do cry a lot, don't they? Sometimes it's hard to have a new baby in the house."

I encouraged her to keep observing his doll play, to continue to connect more deeply with her son. Perhaps when the new baby cries, because the adult must tend to the baby, the attention moves away from the older sibling. How frustrating for the toddler! Yelling at his doll, rather than at the real baby, is a way to help him release his feelings without yelling at his new sibling. It may have been tempting for his mom to say, "That's not nice! We don't shout at babies," which would shut down the opportunity for understanding the impetus behind the behavior.

When my client got curious about her son's play, she discovered a window into what her child was thinking about, so she could empathize with him. Later, when the real baby sleeps, I suggested that Mom say, "I'm still thinking about your dolly crying. Tell me more about that game." This opens the conversation and sets the stage for understanding.

It's always a good idea to offer a doll to any young child, regardless of whether they have a sibling or not. Babies are such a big part of any kid's world because every kid was once a baby. Playing with dolls gives them the opportunity to work out many aspects of their lives, such as nurturing, responsibility, conflict, even how to express love and affection.

The Packing Game

When my children were babies and toddlers, I was fortunate to have a close neighbor, Jenny, with children the same age. We were both full-time caregivers to our children, and we spent a lot of time together as our children played around us. When our eldest children were about four or five, the Packing Game commenced. Jenny and I had a love-hate relationship with the Packing Game. On the one hand, all of the children could play it for hours, but on the other hand, it took forever to clean up this game.

Here's how it worked: The children would find a bag, backpack, or suitcase and proceed to "pack" their small toys, blankies, paper scraps, crayons, etc., into the bags. They'd pack for the park, the beach, or a business trip (my husband frequently traveled overseas for work). Jenny and I would look on in horror, thinking only of the mess of tiny items we would later have to "unpack" and return to their proper spots in our homes.

However, I was fortunate enough to have my early childhood experience tucked in my back pocket and was able to look at this play, not as a form of parental torture, but as a truly exceptional exercise in how the children were processing their experiences. Think about how often you pack and unpack a diaper bag. Consider the thought (and stress) that goes into a trip to the beach with small children. Think about you or your partner heading off for a work trip, leaving the family behind. This play was an important way that our children were making sense of what they saw their grown-ups doing day in and day out. It gave them autonomy and "bigness," as they got to choose which sparkly gem to add to the bag and whether or not they should include a lovey for their little sibling. Snacks? No problem—they'd fill another bag with the plastic food from the play kitchen.

Not only were the kids making sense of their world, but they were also organizing, categorizing, and rehearsing sequences in a way that made the most sense to them. I'd love to tell you that we allowed this game as often as the children wanted to play it, but that's not true. There were many times that we would see it begin to unfold and exasperatedly say, "No Packing Game today!" (And it's okay to put boundaries around your child's play when you know that you don't have the bandwidth for it.)

Superhero Play

Do you have a child who loves superhero play? I know, it can be a bit overwhelming to manage from a parent's perspective: the jumping, shouting, weapon-wielding, and all those large arm motions as they POW the bad guys. But what if you looked at superhero play less as a nuisance or a sign of too much screen time or media influence? What if you looked deeper and saw the purpose of this kind of play?

Come with me back to 2001, when I was teaching in a four-year-old class filled with children who seemed to do nothing but "shoot" each other and cause chaos in the dramatic play area of the classroom. Day after day, the same group of rowdy boys entered the area and stacked up the large, heavy, hollow wooden blocks loudly and with gusto. "Here we go again," I sighed, giving my teaching assistant the nod to head over there and keep things "under control." Despite a classroom meeting on noise levels, despite the pleas from the children who wanted to quietly play family with the dolls and one another, and finally, a visit from a neighboring teacher coming in to tell me that we were being too loud, I knew I had to figure something out.

I was still a newish teacher, but I was experienced enough to know that breaking up the play or separating the children might stop the disruption, but I also knew that these boys were playing about important themes in their development. I had to harness the power of their enthusiasm for superhero play and make it a little more manageable in the classroom, rather than forbidding it. If you try to tell your kids they "can't play" something, they will still do it—maybe not in front of you, but trust me, they'll find a way. You can't make kids not play something they really want to play. So, I sought out the support of my fellow teachers at school and we brainstormed.

"They watch too much TV. Let's say no more superheroes in our class," one teacher suggested.

"It's an outside-only game," suggested another teacher.

"Separate them. It's too much," said another teacher.

"Hold on. Back up," I said. "Let's figure out why this play is so important to them. What are they communicating when they play this way?"

"Feeling powerful!"

"Feeling like a hero! Being the good guy!"

"Using their physical strengths."

Okay, now we were getting somewhere.

When children play superheroes, there are a lot of important things happening. Children, generally speaking, don't get to be the problem solvers in their world. They aren't the ones making big, impactful decisions. It's usually the adults that alter the course of the goings-on. When these children were pretending to be Power Rangers (or Avengers or X-Men or Justice League or whatever it is), they were in charge. With one swipe of an arm and the crash of a big block, they could have a big impact. They needed to feel powerful.

Once we brought this important perspective to the forefront, we were able to come up with some meaningful strategies to support growth and development by working with the children instead of against them. We had a class meeting and pulled out a large piece of oaktag. I sat the children down on the rug and uncapped my marker. "What is the important thing about superheroes?" I asked the class.

They looked up at me and then I saw one little boy, the ringleader of the Power Rangers game, crack a smile. "They have *power!*" he shouted. I wrote it down.

Another child spoke up. "They are strong."

One after another, the children expressed the ways being a superhero made them feel. When the children played Power Rangers, they felt big and important in a world where they usually need support.

I hung the list up in our classroom. The children who were used to being admonished for their rowdy play now felt proud and seen. Their work was important.

We continued to allow superhero play all year. At times, we put limits on it in order to give other children a chance to get into the dramatic play area. At times, we took the superheroes out to the playground and let them have all the blocks to themselves to play superheroes as loudly and boisterously as they wanted to.

We also brainstormed ways to give the children more opportunities to feel powerful in the classroom, besides just through superhero play. We added more ways for them to feel big, like woodworking with real tools. We let them choose whether we would put out big mural paintings or whether we should move the shelves around on certain days, to make more room for an enormous block building.

We voted on snacks and whether we should play outside or in the large playroom at recess. Things still got too rowdy at times, teachers still may have told us to quiet down on some days, but the children's superhero play was recognized and honored for the importance that it held. As a parent, you can reframe your thoughts and knee-jerk reactions about the purpose behind their more boisterous, active, or loud play.

Collecting

Does your child collect pocket treasures? You know, mini piles of lint, random plastic barrettes found on the street, tiny pinecones or pebbles? Dirty, sticky things that look like trash to you?

Hold up! Before you sweep those objects into the garbage, let's think about the purpose of collecting. How is it serving your child? What is important about collecting and what is your little one learning?

Young babies start to categorize animate and inanimate objects as young as three to four months. In toddlerhood, children categorize by color, shape, and size, and in preschool, you'll really start to see collection and categorization explode. Not only are your child's pocket collections supporting their developmental urge to sort and categorize, but collecting items also gives them a sense of ownership and responsibility, as they get to choose what to keep and what to let go of. This keeps their decision-making skills sharp and boosts their self-esteem.

Have you ever been to a beach with sea glass? Where I live, on the North Shore of Boston, there are beautiful pieces of smooth colorful glass on the beaches, especially at low tide. When my children were small, one of our favorite summer activities was to go on sea glass walks where we would collect these beautiful treasures. Originally glass bottles that had been littered into the sea by passing boats, these bits of glass were tossed around in the ocean for years, breaking into parts and smoothing into frosted stones. We called these "keepers."

Occasionally, we found still-sharp sea glass. We called them "throwbacks." The sea had not finished smoothing them. Giving the children a category for what we could keep and what we had to throw back gave them a way to be detectives in charge of the treasure, and it gave them a limit and framework for what was and was not allowed.

You can use the same concept for found treasures with your child. Define some boundaries around what can be kept, and involve your child in the discussion. A Band-Aid, a sharp object, or something they may choke on can be a throwback (or put in the garbage) and everything else can be a keeper. It is okay for you to decide that something is unsanitary or unsafe and not to be kept. It is okay for your child to be upset about it. Before you get overwhelmed imagining your home filled with bits of yarn and shiny gum wrappers, don't worry. I have a system for you.

Find a pouch or a sturdy box. Let them fill it up and keep their special items inside. Once the box or pouch is full, have them dump it all out and sort through it. They get to decide what stays and what goes in order to make room for the new treasures. If you are feeling especially crafty, have them decorate the pouch or box, showing them you also value their findings. Keep the pouch in a special place. Having a treasure box or pouch will allow you to honor your child's interests while also honoring your own space as a parent. You may also notice that when your child does dump out their box, you will get interesting insights into their interests. Is your child's box full of snail and cicada shells, random tool bits, pinecones and acorns, or brightly colored shiny and sparkly things? These collections can give you unique insights into what your child is thinking about.

Playing Dead

"Lizzie, my kindergartner keeps playing 'dead and alive,' and now my preschooler wants to play, too. I'm scared they'll do it at school! What should I do?"

I had just sat down on my couch and was drinking a steaming cup of coffee before my own kids trickled in from school, when I received this direct message in my Instagram inbox. I knew my answer would help this parent feel calmer about her kids pretending to be dead, a common game for children of this age.

Seeing children play about being dead can bring up complicated feelings for parents, and I want to reassure you that most of the time, playing dead is a healthy sign of cognitive development. Playing "dead and alive" allows children to work out complex ideas about what those words mean, in a safe and controlled way.

Death, even for adults, can be a scary abstract concept, so you can imagine that as children learn about it, they're going to need to play about it. Get curious. Later on (not during the play), ask them, "I noticed you were playing about being dead today. That's so interesting. Tell me more about that . . ." You could also say, "Lots of five-year-olds are figuring out about what it means to be dead. Do you have any questions about that?"

My typical way of explaining what dead means to kids is the following, but you should make it make sense for your family's beliefs: "Dead means that a body stops working. The heart stops pumping blood, and the brain doesn't think anymore. When someone or something is dead, they are dead forever. In a game or on TV, you might see characters wake up or look like they are sleeping, but that is just pretend. Different people think about dying in different ways and lots of people feel sad or scared about that. It's okay to feel however you feel. Do you have questions?" Remember that all play serves a purpose, so when you start to feel overwhelmed or worried by your child's play, come back to the purpose and go from there.

Making Potions, Experiments, or Recipes

When I was a kid, I remember sneaking, with my sister, into the bathroom when we were supposed to be asleep for the night. We'd take a few paper Dixie cups off the stack meant for rinsing our mouths after brushing our teeth, and line them up on the counter, pretending to be on a cooking show in the dimly lit mirror of the gray bathroom. We'd fill each cup with shampoos, lotions, soaps, anything we could find in the bathroom, without making a sound. The trick was that we couldn't add water because if we turned on the faucet, our parents would hear us up there, and the jig would be up!

We'd spend hours making various recipes, pretending to eat and drink them on our "cooking show." I must've been about eight or nine at the time, and I cannot remember if we ever got caught, but I can remember how much fun we had making those concoctions and then stealthily cleaning them up before returning to our beds.

Many, many years later with three young children of my own, I was excited to set up a potion-making station for them to discover when they awoke from their afternoon naps and quiet time. I set out a water dispenser, a few bowls, spoons, whisks, and an old medicine dropper. I filled squeeze bottles with water and food coloring, then added glitter to a few of them. That afternoon, I set up a snack outside on the deck and watched the children play with potions for a long lazy afternoon at home.

Each child turned the play into what they needed it to be. My son, who loves precision, spent time measuring and squirting exact amounts, even going inside to get the measuring spoons from the kitchen. My middle daughter mixed colors for a pretend smoothie shop with my youngest daughter. They used intentional and exciting language to describe the smoothies they were making, like "Silly Strawberry."

Not only were they learning scientific concepts like measurement and volume, but they were also honing fine motor skills through pouring and stirring. Most importantly, they were gaining self-confidence and learning patience as they negotiated over ideas and materials with one another. While they played and bickered and played some more, I thought about how much they were getting out of this kind of play—so similar to the game my sister and I played on the sly so many years before.

While I am not recommending that you let your kids make potions out of expensive toiletries under the cloak of night, I am saying that next time you see your kids pouring the salt into a cup of water, perhaps suggest a version of the potion station that you feel is manageable. As the parent or caregiver, it is up to you to decide what feels manageable to you.

For example, your four-year-old is sitting at the dinner table making a potion from their food and the salt and pepper shakers. That would be a hard no for me. I would not be okay with them using the food I had prepared as potion ingredients just because it is important for them to play. Instead, I would say something like, "It looks like you want to mix things up to make something new. I can't let you use our dinner food for experiments, but I can put together some potion ingredients for another day. Let's talk about what ingredients you might want to use while we finish up dinner and get ready for bath time."

Your job is to set boundaries around what you are comfortable with. Involving your child in the planning for another day will help them see that you understand that potion making is fun and important! Later in this book, I will show you how to set up physical boundaries around play to keep the mess contained.

The intention here is not to psychoanalyze everything your children do. In the spirit of observation, looking with curiosity rather than judgment at the way your child is playing simply helps you to see them for the creative, capable, and interesting humans they are. It can boost your confidence in your child's ability to play independently, and it can help you to appreciate what they are learning and what they might need from you in terms of support and understanding. Trust that however they are playing, growth and development are happening and they are benefiting—even when you can't for the life of you figure out what their purpose is.

8

BARRIERS TO PLAY

Whether the concept of independent play overwhelms you or seems doable, the fact is that there will always be barriers to achieving the family schedule, structure, or dynamic you are aiming for. All children will require the support of a caring adult to build the habit of and protect their independent play. Our current culture doesn't support the time and space to build solid play habits, and so, it will become your job to ensure that the culture of your family supports your child's play routine.

Whether your child is easygoing and drawn to independent play or you have a "stage-five clinger," instituting a solid independent play routine will always take work. Let's go through some of the obstacles you may face and how to overcome them as you work to integrate a new system into your household and a new level of consciousness into your parenting.

How to Encourage Independent Play

Before I get into how you can actually be a barrier to your child's play, I want to be clear again that it's perfectly fine and normal to want to play with your child sometimes. Just because you are instituting a new routine of independent play doesn't mean you have to be totally out of the play picture, unless you want to be. But for most people, playing with their child is the main way they connect.

That's okay. You can use play as a way to connect with your child. It's fine. Don't overthink it. Of course you can play with your kid. Sometimes you will be your child's playmate. The point is not to do this all the time. It is up to you to decide how much you'll play with your child, but the point of this book is to *also* have an independent play routine in your home where you get time to yourself. It's a balance.

What matters is understanding when you might be interfering with your child's play process. Be aware in your own mind about the difference between playing with your child, observing and narrating your child's play, and letting your child play independently. At each of these levels, you can let your child lead the play, or you can accidentally take over.

Your child might like this, especially if they aren't yet used to playing independently and that is your typical play mode. It's familiar. Your child likes it when you entertain them. But if you want them to play independently, I want to give you some guidance on how to step back and encourage your child to take the lead.

"Sportscasting" Your Child's Play

Imagine you are a parent playing with your young toddler in your child's room. There are books on a bookshelf, a soft cozy carpet to sit on, and various bins and buckets filled with balls, blocks, stuffed animals, and toys that rattle and shake. Now imagine your child pulls a plastic red barn from the bin. They grip the handle with their chubby hands and pull until the barn and animals come free. You sit down beside them and start to play "barn" with them.

If you are like most parents, your instinct is likely to ask your child, "What sound does this sheep make?" and then cheer excitedly when they respond, "Baa." You might lead the chicks into the barn and pretend to feed them. Your child will probably be happy to follow your ideas. It is likely they'll love the connection and attention you are providing, not to mention the wonderful ways in which you are benefiting their language development and other skills.

But what if you could play alongside them in a way that would teach them how to play independently in the future? What if you let their ideas lead the play, not yours? What if you could give them the connection, attention, and language support they need throughout the day, while allowing play to become exclusively their work?

A useful approach for transitioning out of being your child's playmate is to use the reflective or narrative technique we've talked about before. You will still be right there with your child, participating in the play, but you are slowly withdrawing your influence on the play by letting them lead. You do what they do or describe what they are doing. You'll still support them, but you won't lead their play. Think of yourself as your child's mirror, or like a sportscaster, narrating the game as your child plays.

Parenting expert Janet Lansbury, known for her respectful

parenting approach, has made "sportscasting" popular among parents today, but the technique actually comes from earlier parenting expert Magda Gerber, who believed in watching and describing children's activities without interfering too much.

Here's how this technique might look, using the example of the barn toy.

Your child pulls out the barn and animals. You sit nearby and wait to see what your child will do, instead of jumping right into a game or questions. Maybe they will begin to move the sheep around. Instead of giving them ideas about what to do next—which you will likely be tempted to do, especially if your child seems uncertain—simply copy their actions. As they move the sheep around, you move another animal around in the same way. If they start making sheep noises, you make them, too. Let them be the leader, and you follow them.

If they put the sheep inside the barn, you do it, too. If they make the sheep fly up to the roof of the barn, you do it, too. Rather than initiating an idea like feeding the sheep or taking the "flying sheep" idea to the next level by making it fly around in the sky, try saying, "The sheep is in the barn now." Then, if they choose, let them sit in silence. You don't have to make anything a teachable moment or fill in the gaps of their play. Believe that your child knows what they are doing, and watch them do it.

This is harder than it sounds if you are used to directing the play. This scenario likely feels familiar: You pick up a toy in your child's playroom, a marble run. You say, "Look what this does!" as you demonstrate. You hand the marble to your child. "Here, do it like this. Make it go down the track! No, like this. No, no, put your hand like this. There, good job! You did it!" This kind of play feels satisfying to adults because they taught their child how to do something—but if you want your child's play to feel satisfying to *them,* and you want independent play to become a good habit, self-discovery (vs. parent teaching) is what will give them the feeling of satisfaction.

Dictating how your child interacts with their toys can inadvertently do the opposite of what you initially intended. This is the barrier. Consistently "teaching" your child how to use their toys takes away the opportunity for self-discovery and self-mastery. When we say, "Look at this," or "Do it that way," we remove their chance to explore, learn, and discover on their own terms. Stay out of the driver's seat of your child's play and instead become an engaged passenger who is along for a beautiful ride.

Rather than pointing your child to the marble run and telling them what to do, try pulling it to the front and center of the room. Wait and watch them notice it and observe them as they check it out. If and when they look to you, respond with encouragement and narrate your observations aloud. "You're noticing the marble run I pulled out. I saw you carefully running your finger along the side..."

They are the play experts. They learn how to initiate their own ideas, without an adult to lean on, building play confidence and frustration tolerance as they set their own goals and try to meet them. It may drive you crazy seeing your child working a toy in the "wrong" way, but take a deep breath, hold back, and see what happens.

Other Ways to Step Back

Here are some more ways to shift your role in your child's play from barrier to bridge:

- Instead of holding a toy up for your baby and shaking it for them and saying, "Look! Look! It's making noise," try placing the toy in front of them and observing how they interact with it. Remember to narrate: "You're pushing it, and it's rolling!"

- Your three-year-old wants you to play the puppy in the game, so you make barking noises and entertain her, making her laugh. Instead, try asking, "What will the puppy do in the game? Tell me more about your ideas."

- Your child wants you to draw with them, so you take out a piece of paper and start making hearts and rainbows. Instead, try waiting to see how they are drawing, and mimic their ideas. "You're making blue lines. I'm going to try that, too."

Remember my story about my daughter counting out grapes two by two, instead of counting to higher numbers? I wanted to jump right in and correct her, until I realized that her goal was not the same as mine. Parents have an impulse to control what the child is doing because in so many ways we have to do that, but barring a child doing something dangerous or inappropriate (or causing a giant mess you don't want to clean up), play is one area where you can let go of the reins.

When you set out a toy for your child and stand back, they may not even be interested in the toy at all because they have some other play agenda, and that's fine, too. In fact, that's great because it means they are already thinking for themselves and relying on their own ideas. The more you show your children that you value their ideas and are interested in seeing where they will go with their play, the more they'll learn to recognize themselves as autonomous. They'll build play confidence and their independent play skills will grow exponentially.

Other Barriers to Independent Play

You are an important support system for your child's play. You are not the President of Play. Back off, observe, narrate, and be curious instead. See how narration and reflection change the dynamic. This is less about the play itself than it is about honoring and recognizing who your child is through their play.

Here are some other ways parents can become barriers to play without realizing they are doing it.

Feeling Guilty

Don't underestimate its power! Guilt is common and insidious for many reasons, one of which is that it can become a barrier to independent play. Parents may try to compensate for their perceived parenting faults in all kinds of ways. Guilt can make parents behave in ways that are misaligned with our values around play. Parents might play with their children more than they would like, give in to more screen time than they believe is right, or buy every toy the child wants on a whim. That's not to say that there is anything intrinsically wrong with playing with your child, allowing screen time, buying toys, or getting kids into activities. These can all be fun and special parts of life, but they can also become barriers to play.

Guilt is tricky for everyone, but play doesn't need to be guilt-inducing. When the guilt creeps in and you think, "Shouldn't I play with them?" or "I feel bad saying no," I want you to remember that you are making an intentional choice to help your child build independent play skills. Not playing with them every time they ask is part of the program. Connect with them throughout the day, be playful, but don't let guilt dictate that you play with them. You are breaking down barriers to independent play. Guiltily playing when you really don't want to builds barriers.

Interrupting

How often do you start something, get interrupted, and then wonder what you were even doing in the first place? It's frustrating. Kids feel the same way when we disrupt their play with suggestions and questions. If your child is in the flow of play, save your comments for later. They don't need you to narrate or ask questions when they are in it.

- Reconnect on their play ideas at dinnertime. "Luca, today I noticed you working on a tall and skinny block building in the playroom. There was a line of red cubes leading from the bottom of the building over to your dinosaurs. I am so curious about that!"

- Wonder aloud about their play ideas while they get ready for bed. "Sammy, I can't stop thinking about those leaves you collected at the playground. It looked like you were looking for a certain kind. What were you thinking about when you collected them?"

If you want your children to get more invested in their own thoughts and ideas, show them that you care, too . . . just not while they are playing. Of course, you won't do this all the time. You'll interrupt sometimes, and that is okay! But the more we refer to our children as the experts on their own play, the more they'll own that identity.

Lacking Confidence

Yet another barrier is a lack of confidence that your child will be capable of independent play—or *you* will be capable of being consistent enough to implement an independent play routine. Trust me and my experience when I tell you that every child is capable of independent play. Not every child will play independently in the same way, but they can all do it, if you give them the space, the environment, and the support. As for you, just remember that creating an atmosphere conducive to independent play in your home takes a little more work up front and commitment to some new habits. After new routines are established, play becomes much *less* work for you, and your life will become easier because you'll have more time to do all the things you need to do. That includes relaxing and taking care of yourself. You can do this.

"Saving" Your Child from Frustration

Part of playing independently is dealing with frustration that an involved adult might have prevented. Not preventing your child's frustration is actually a good thing—children who build frustration tolerance are better able to deal with problems and persevere, but it's really difficult not to intervene when you see your child struggling.

Let's say your child is happily building with blocks, and then their baby sibling toddles over and knocks it over. In a flash, their building is decimated. They explode with anger. Looking up and seeing your crying baby and angry preschooler, you may say, "What's gotten into you? It's not that big of a deal. Why are you so upset? Don't give up. Just build it again."

Now let's reframe this situation. Imagine you've folded an entire basket of laundry, and your child comes along and knocks it over. All the folded clothes are now lying in a wrinkled heap. You spent so much time doing that! You explode with frustration, and your partner says, "It's not a big deal, honey. Don't get so upset. Just fold it again." You would lose your mind, right?

Your child needs you to know and acknowledge how they feel. Try, "Gosh, that really stinks. You worked really hard on that, and your little sister knocked it down. Now you have a huge mess. You know what? Let's figure out what to do."

You can sit in it with them, and then they can choose what to do about the problem. "Do you want to clean it up and start again? Do you want to do something else and come back to this later?" You can help them scaffold their thinking in order to work through the problem, while still allowing them to be the one to decide what to do about it.

Frustration is an opportunity for mindfulness, thinking, learning, and problem-solving for your child. Not solving your child's frustration also makes your life as a parent so much easier because every mishap isn't your problem. It's your child's problem to solve. You are just the support system.

Note: Most children cannot take in a lot of language when they are upset. Wait until they are calm, even if that's much later, to have this conversation. It is always okay to revisit an old mishap. Don't try to teach while they are upset.

Environmental Barriers

Is your environment set up for independent play?

Think about your child and how they exist in your home environment. What's the easiest thing to do? Watch a screen? Follow you around? Do the play opportunities available to your child require your intervention or assistance? In chapter 10, I'll go into

MODELING FRUSTRATION TOLERANCE

One of the best ways to build frustration tolerance in children is by modeling your own management of frustrating feelings. Let's say you burned the toast. You can say, "Oh no! I burned the toast! I really wish I hadn't burned the toast. Now I am so mad! What am I going to do? Hmm. I could make a new piece of toast. Or, I could have something different for breakfast." This is how you model that problem-solving of frustration.

Maybe you are in line at the grocery store. You can say out loud to your kid, "It is so hard to wait! I really wish the line would hurry up but it's not going to. This is so hard for me. I need to think about what I can do when it's really hard for me to wait." They take in these lessons. When you model frustration tolerance, you give your kids skills.

more detail about how to set up your home (no matter its size) for independent play, and how easy it is—easier, in fact, than constantly having to help facilitate a game, a craft, or a building project.

Another environmental barrier, ironically, can be too many toys. Chapter 14 is all about toys, but you can start right now thinking about whether toy clutter keeps your child from easily accessing the toys that spark their imagination right now. There are easy and satisfying ways to cut through the clutter and curate toys that are both interesting to your child personally and conducive to independent play.

Scheduling Barriers

Instead of conditioning kids to hustle more and push harder, what would happen if we valued time to play and rest? What would it feel like to reserve time for the playground instead of the lessons? What would the result be if we worried less about kids being at the top of the class and more about kids feeling comfortable in their own skin? Adults may have a hard time relaxing and feeling grounded, but kids already know the answer is time for play. All we need to do is provide them that time.

I do want to be sensitive to the fact that different families have varying childcare needs, and many parents require childcare while they work. Some families don't have access to safe green space for their children to play and they use after-school activities as a way to keep their children out of harm's way. I want to be clear that the ideas in this section are meant to empower parents, not shame anyone for their choices.

When my kids were small, I was a stay-at-home mom. Not only were lots of sports and classes not in my budget, but it was important for me to protect their unscheduled downtime. While I wanted my kids to be exposed to valuable sports and lessons, I also wanted them to relax and have the opportunity to run around in the neighborhood and have as much unstructured playtime as possible. Leaving afternoons open was my goal.

During the school day, kids are told when to sit, where to walk, and how to learn. It's structured down to the minute. At home, I felt that my job was to provide the balance. They loved that open-ended, wandering, play-with-whoever-turns-up, creative, child-led downtime. It was within that space that they learned to listen to their internal rhythms and figure out how to be. It also made our family life simpler, easier, and less expensive.

Now that my kids are older, I work from home. I have less free time to spend supporting their play. They have more homework, and they've decided to play team sports. Their needs have changed and so have our family's needs. While we are much busier these days, we all look back fondly on those dance-to-the-beat-of-your-own-drum afternoons from many years back.

When the school year begins each fall and sign-ups loom, you and your kids have a choice about how busy they will be. As you think about what kind of schedule you'd like your children to have, as well as what kind of care and supervision options are necessary for your family, you and your child can work together to make choices about their potential activities.

Be honest about how each activity feels and how it will fit into your lives. The goal isn't to eliminate all structured activities. It's about finding the right balance for your family.

That might mean embracing a full schedule of activities that also provide childcare. For others, it could mean fiercely protecting unscheduled time. Working parents might need to rely more on structured after-school programs. Some after-school programs are loosely structured and can provide kids with some time for independent play, but more often, the environment is pretty controlled. Families with neurodivergent children might find that certain structured activities provide essential support and routine, while still ensuring some flexibility for decompression.

Even with a lot of daily structure, you can still prioritize pockets of free time on the weekends, depending on your schedule. Check in regularly with yourself and your child. Are they feeling overscheduled? Are they getting enough playtime? Are the activities they are in sustainable and bringing more joy than stress?

There is no perfect formula, only the one that works best for your family right now. That formula will change as your children grow, work situations shift, and new opportunities arrive. So whether your child's afternoons are filled with sports practices, music lessons, therapeutic activities, unstructured play, or a mix of all of these, what matters most is that your choices align with your family's values, support your child's development, and contribute to a mostly balanced family life.

MANAGING SCREEN TIME

Before we dive into the topic of screen time—one of the most common concerns of parents these days—it is important to know that I am not anti-screen. In today's modern world, zero screen time feels unrealistic to me. I consider my approach low-screen, not anti-screen. My own children enjoy time on screens, as do I, and I don't feel guilty about it. It is your job as a parent to decide how much screen time and what kind of screen time is appropriate for your child. I can help you with the balance of play and screens, but you are the one who gets to decide what feels good to you and for your family.

People often ask me how much screen time I allowed my children at various ages, and my answer remains the same: It doesn't matter. Each child and family is different and what was appropriate for my child won't be the same for your child.

Before reading this book, you may have equated your child's play with entertainment. Now, you know better. Play has a much more serious purpose. In the words of Fred Rogers, from his book

You Are Special: Neighborly Words of Wisdom from Mister Rogers, "Play is often talked about as if it were a relief from serious learning. But for children, play *is* serious learning. Play is really the work of childhood."

It's harder to play than to be passively entertained. A child who is used to constantly being entertained may struggle to play independently at first. Passive entertainment can be fun and easy (and sometimes necessary), but it is often a barrier to play. And there is no more fun, easy, and accessible form of entertainment for kids as well as adults than screen time.

What I mean by screen time is any time spent looking at an electronic screen, including watching videos and television shows, playing video games, and using a tablet, computer, or phone. We could spend time hashing out the differences and statistics between passive viewing, interactive viewing, video games, etc., but for the purpose of giving you the clarity and knowledge to make firm, clear decisions in your home, I am going to regard all screen time as having the same value.

A popular 2024 book called *The Anxious Generation* cited the science behind the mental health costs of too much screen time, and it sent a ripple of anxiety through parents. Many who read this book had their worst fears about screen time confirmed. A quick Google search on screen time and kids will yield some pretty scary, guilt-inducing results. We already know that kids are on screens more than ever before. We live in a time where we are all overscheduled, exhausted, and bombarded by options to tune out the world with the flick of a power button.

But I want you to know this: You can have children who both love screens and love to play independently without them.

Screens are addictive. They're designed that way. The fast-paced TV shows and video games our kids watch and play are made to trigger the brain's reward systems. Programmers of shows and games know what makes children tick, and they have a deep scientific and technological understanding of how to keep a child hooked. A three-year-old watching *Daniel Tiger's Neighborhood* or *Bluey* is mesmerized because those shows reflect their life experiences, and those writers understand child development.

Think back to before your children were born. I bet you had some pretty sturdy opinions about screen time and kids. I know I sure did. I used to think things like:

"I'll never let my kids use screens at a restaurant."

"I would never allow screens in the car!"

"No screens before the age of three for my kids!"

When my oldest child was born (he's about to go off to college now), I really thought he wouldn't watch screens until at least two. I was a preschool teacher! I have a master's degree in early childhood ed! I was sure that if anyone was going to keep her kids from getting sucked into screens, it was going to be me.

Spoiler alert: He was a big fan of *Sesame Street* and *Thomas the Tank Engine & Friends* well before his second birthday.

Little by little, screens have crept into our lives. It started with cell phones and portable DVD players. Now even elementary school kids often have cell phones, and administrators hand out tablets in school. We've integrated screen time so deeply into our lives and the lives of our children that many people forget they have a choice about where, when, what, and how much screen time is consumed in their family.

During the pandemic, between virtual schooling and surviving working from home with no childcare, screen time became even more prevalent. High levels of parental stress are associated with significantly more hours of media screen time in children, and I think it's safe to say *all* parents experienced high levels of stress during the pandemic. (If you are nodding along and feeling guilty about screen time for your child during the pandemic, I want to pause for a second. You raised a child in a pandemic, so let's acknowledge that accomplishment, drop the guilt, and learn some ways to rebalance the scale now.)

The good news? You do not have to be afraid. You are an informed parent who values your child's play and is ready to take control of how they spend their time, on screens and off. I believe that when used intentionally, and with firm limits and boundaries, screens can be a useful and enjoyable tool in your parenting arsenal. With some clear intention and strategies, you can learn to make screens work *for* you and not against you.

In parenting, you can always start over, exactly where you are in the moment. It's never too late to begin a new routine or recalibrate what you're doing. Don't worry—you haven't messed up your kids, even if they currently spend a lot of time on screens. We can teach our children (and ourselves) how to regulate screen use. Take a deep breath, exhale, and let go of what your family's screen time may or may not have looked like over the past few years. Nothing is fixed. You can set limits now, and you can learn how to stick to them.

Finding Screen Time Balance

Think about your family's dynamic with screens. How often do you feel stressed about your child's consumption of screens? Do you get in power struggles with your child around this issue? Have you tried to set strict screen time rules before, then given up on them and regretted it? Maybe you've even lied to yourself about how much time your family spends on screens, or purposefully *not* tallied it up out of fear of what you'll find. That last one gets me. I know that when I feel like I am avoiding thinking about it, it's time to recalibrate.

The real problem isn't the screen time. The real problem develops when screen time is used as a default instead of a tool. Using screen time as a tool in parenting is not only possible, but it can be beneficial. But before we get into parenting strategies, let's take a look at what, for you and your family, might feel like a healthy balance of screen time versus other activities.

If you wave a magic wand and manage screens exactly the way you wanted with no effort, what would that look like? Every family's relationship with screens will be different. To me, an overall healthy balance means that your kids can enjoy screen time, but it doesn't replace their inner drive to play, make, and create. Children can use screen time for intentional enjoyment, rather than a default behavior (such as waking up and turning the TV on, or walking in the door and turning on the iPad, or getting in the car and immediately turning on shows in the back seat). Children can use screens and also play and work productively. You can have both—with consistency and intention you can do it.

If you want to limit screen time, here is your job description:

- **It is your job** to decide how much screen time and what kind of screen time is appropriate for your child.

- **It is your job** to stay firm and calm when your child is asking for screens. You don't have to convince them out of wanting more screens by telling them why or how bad screens are. You do have to tell them if, when, and where screens will be available to them.

- **It is your job** to be in charge of tablets, remotes, and devices. Just like locking the doors to your home and insisting on wearing seat belts, you can put away screens to keep your family safe. Children do not benefit from unfettered access to the online world.

- **It is your child's job** to push back, ask for more, and check if you are truly able to hold your limit. They are not bad for wanting more. It's great that you've raised them to feel comfortable asking for what they want.

The world on the screen can supersede the work of creating their own world, but the screens do the work, which, if overused, can override the desire to play outside, interact with friends, and participate in other recreational activities.

Sometimes, circumstances will present when the goal needs to be different. Perhaps there's a new baby or a parent has fallen ill. Maybe there's a lockdown, or they are staying with a grandparent. In those cases, the short-term screen time goal might be different than the overall long-term goal, and that's OKAY. When the goal is an *overall balance*, temporary circumstances in which kids spend more time on screens will be balanced out by times when they spend less time on screens. The trick is not to let those temporary times become the norm.

Finding that balance is possible.

When my children were small—three, six, and eight—I used to drive the long haul with them between New Jersey and Massachusetts, to and from my in-laws' house at the beach. I was the only adult in the car. The trip took six hours on a good day. The first few times, I was determined to not let them watch iPads the whole time. I wanted them to look out the window, rest, listen to music, etc. I was really stuck on being able to make the trip without screens. Guess what happened?

By the time we arrived at our destination, I was exhausted from concentrating on driving while also working to keep three children occupied in the back seat. I was answering all their questions, changing the music and podcast selections, managing bickering and crying, and keeping the older ones quiet when the little one finally fell asleep. When we got where we were going, I was wrecked. I couldn't be the present or patient mom I wanted to be.

As I grew as a parent and learned to set goals and be intentional, I learned that screens on that long solo drive were a really important tool for our family. Once I allowed the screens to be used more freely in this specific setting, I was able to relax a bit on the long drive. I could listen to my own podcast or audiobooks, concentrate on directions, and the distractions were a lot fewer. When we arrived at our destination, I was less wrecked from the drive, and I could delight in our arrival with my kids. Screens on that drive became a treat the kids and I all looked forward to. It was a treat *because they didn't get to look at screens all the time.*

So how do you get from here to there—from your family's current screen usage to the healthy balance you desire? Here are five ideas to lean on:

1. The adult is in charge of screen time.
2. The adult says when, what, and how much screen time.
3. When not in use, devices stay up high and out of sight.
4. Program the media that you feel good about and delete the other options from the device.
5. Give warnings and follow through. Accept feelings around wanting more, but don't change your mind and offer more.

How to Make—and Keep—Screen Boundaries

There is *nothing* simple about setting up screen time limits and boundaries. So, I want to introduce to you what I call the "Always Sometimes" Method.

This method will allow you to set intentional limits and boundaries on screen time and allow for flexibility when you need it most. It sounds like this:

- "You can **always** watch your shows on Saturday and Sunday mornings. You can count on that. **Sometimes**, you'll have an extra show or two during the week. That's a grown-up choice, not a child choice."

- "You can **always** watch your shows in the morning while you have your milk and Mom gets ready for work. You can count on that. **Sometimes**, we watch a movie together after the bath. That's a grown-up choice, not a child choice."

- "You can **always** watch your show when I am making dinner, you can count on that. **Sometimes**, you'll get to watch an extra show after naps. That's a grown-up choice, not a child choice."

This approach works because you are making sure your child knows you are not taking away screen time, just moving things around. They know when they *can* expect it, and they know when they *might* get it, but with a clear understanding that the "sometimes" decisions are not theirs to make. Your child will be able to predict when and where they watch, and when they get used to the new routine, there will be a lot less begging and whining about screens.

You can even make a visual to help your children understand, by making pictures of their routines throughout the day, showing where screens will and will not be on the schedule. When they ask for screens, you can refer them to their chart. The chart shows it's not screen time. That takes away the power struggle because the schedule is enforcing the rules, not the parent.

This method is not a magic formula that when implemented will work perfectly and solve all your screen time worries. Your child will push back. You will doubt yourself and the method. Anytime you make a great change in your life there will be challenges and doubts. That's how you know you're on the right track. When you start a new routine or choose to set new limits and boundaries, I always recommend taking time to decide why you are doing this. Write it down. Ask yourself:

- Why is limiting screen time a goal?
- What is driving my decision to make a change now?
- How will my child benefit from this change?
- Why is this change beneficial for our family as a whole?
- What do I want my family's screen time to look like now? What do I want it to look like in the future? Why?
- What specific behaviors or issues have I noticed that are prompting this change?
- How does our current screen time routine affect my child?
- How will changing our screen time habits impact our daily routines and family dynamics?
- What challenges do I anticipate in implementing these changes?
- What positive outcomes am I hoping to see in my child and in our family relationships?

Be honest with yourself. Dig deep and consider both the short-term adjustments and the long-term benefits you're aiming for. Keep your reasons handy in the Notes app on your phone or on a sticky note in the kitchen. Having a good understanding of the *why* behind your limits will serve as your backbone when you start to doubt yourself.

Preparing for New Screen Time Limits

Putting limits on screens might sound sudden or even mean from your child's perspective. They won't understand or even be interested in all the research into why screen time needs to be regulated. You don't need to tell them screens are bad. Instead of looking at screens as the enemy, engage your child in a conversation about their favorite shows. Let them know that you value what they value. Ask what they love about their shows or games. Who is their favorite character and why? Who do they wish they could be like? Let them get really into it.

Also share what you love about screens for yourself. Do you enjoy relaxing with a movie? Are you a gamer? Share your love with your child so they can see that you don't judge them but share their enjoyment of screens. What was your favorite show when you were your child's age? Share about that.

Send the message that it is okay to enjoy screens for entertainment. This is not about demonizing something your child enjoys. Take away the shame or guilt by connecting with something that they love. You want your children to see that you care about their preferences, and you understand that they love screen time and that you won't take it away from them. You want them to trust that you partner with them to be intentional about screens.

Then, you can say, "We are going to try a new way of using screen time in our house." Depending on how old they are, you might describe how screens are becoming a tricky thing in your house, and you want that to change. "Does it sometimes feel like you are begging for screens, and I am getting so mad? Do you wish you knew exactly when you could watch so that we don't have to argue about it anymore?"

Then, explain the new method. The "Always Sometimes" Method is straightforward and easy for children to understand. Tell them that you are still learning with them. Explain that it is the grown-up's choice when to watch, but the child's choice of what to watch (within limits of what is programmed).

Now, what should you do if your child refuses, or screams and cries about it? Don't panic! Try to stay calm and remember that children learn to accept limits by testing limits. When you set a limit, this time with screens, *it is your child's job to test the limit to make sure it holds.* When your child is carrying on, and this method does not produce immediate results, remember that your child and you are going through a process of putting a new routine in place.

Imagine this: You are about to let your child float in a tube in the deep end of the pool. You blow up the tube and then you test it. You push it under water and make sure it floats to the top. You'll look all around the seams to make sure they are sturdy. If you think you see a weak spot, you might poke at it to make sure it'll hold your child as they float through the water.

Children do the same thing with limits. They must make sure the limit will hold before they can completely let go and trust you. Here are some tools to make this transition a little easier when your child protests:

- **Try empathy.** "I know how hard this is for you. You *wish* you could watch screens all day. I get it! I wish I could, too."

- **Give a choice.** "When this show is over, it will be time to turn off the iPad and put it away. Do you want to be in charge of powering it down, or should I do it for you? Do you want to get the stool and put it away or should I lift you up high to put it in the cabinet?"

- **Set up for next time.** "It's hard to stop watching this movie! Let's write down which movie you were watching and what time it stopped so that tomorrow during screen time, you can start watching from that spot if you choose to."

- **Assert your loving authority.** "You wish I would let you watch, and I am not going to. It is my job to make rules about screens, and I always do my job."

Use what you know about your child to anticipate how they'll react to a new screen time routine. Prepare yourself to stay steady when they do not. Take a few moments and write down your predictions, and then work through how you ideally want to respond (using the strategies in this chapter). When and if your child has a hard time, you can respond with the strategies you prepared instead of reacting in the moment.

One morning, my daughter was going into school late. She excitedly asked me if she could watch shows before it was time to go. She had a whole plan. She would eat breakfast and then chill in front of the fireplace and watch TV until it was time to get ready. It was very sweet and sounded delightful.

Did I say yes? Nope. Did she say, "Okay, Mom, sure, no problem." No way. She stomped around, told me all her friends have phones (not true), and why wouldn't I even let her watch shows before school?

Here's what I didn't say (but I wanted to): "That's not true! Your friends do not have phones. Screens are bad for you and it's bad enough you're on them at school. You have to listen to me! Don't be rude."

Here is what I did say, "That sounds delightful and cozy. I wish I could do that, too! But today is Thursday, and in our home, screens are not available during the week. This weekend, I'll remind you of this cozy plan." Then I went upstairs to make my bed and get dressed and when I came down, she had pulled a little table in front of the fire and was coloring. I wanted to compliment her ingenuity, but I sensed it might make her mad (she's eleven and lots of things that I do make her mad), so instead, I made my coffee and went about my business. I didn't make it my job to entertain her or make her feel good about my choices. I am her parent, and she does not need to approve my decisions.

Later, at dinnertime, I pulled out one of the drawings she was working on and asked her to tell me more about it. My intention was to feel out whether or not she wanted to talk more about her screen time rules. Unsurprisingly, she told me about her drawing and shrugged off the opportunity to complain more about screens. The moral of the story is that children crave limits. Limits help them feel safe and cared for. They'll never say, "Mom, thanks for the limits."

You can see how it was hard for me as well as her to stay calm around that boundary. What can you do when *your* resolve weakens or you feel pushed to the brink? To make boundary setting easier on you, avoid trying to reason with your child. Keep it clear and brief. Kids can't take in a lecture or long explanations when they are processing big emotions. You don't have to convince them that you are right. Now is not the time for screens, period. Tell them when it will be time and move on. Just like you make choices about sleep, food, and hygiene without convincing them you are right, you can make choices about screen time.

"BUT MY FRIENDS GET MORE SCREEN TIME!"

Children from five to teens may counter your rules with the arguments that their friends get more screen time or have fewer limits on screen time, and "that's not fair." Parents get really tripped up trying to explain this. They often default to "screens are bad!" and then get trapped in a power struggle. I have a simple response to this. Calmly say, "It's true, some of your friends are allowed, and you're not. That is hard. Different families have different rules for many different reasons. It might not feel fair to you. In our house, this is the way we do screen time."

Practicing the Limits Ahead of Time

Another way to help children adjust to the new routine is to practice the routine before you have to enforce it. Imagine your child is happily settling onto the couch, snack in hand, ready to flip the iPad to their favorite show. You are looking forward to an hour of quiet. You deserve it! But then you anticipate the end of iPad time—the part where you need to physically pry the iPad out of your screaming child's hand. It is exhausting. You know you need to stick to the original limit, but it is so tempting to just let them keep watching. The fight doesn't feel worth it. What can you do? You solve this problem before it starts.

Before you hand over the iPad, tell them, "When the clock says 3:00 p.m. (point to the 3 on the clock), it will tell us that it's time for the iPad to be turned off and put away. Even if you wish you could watch more, and even if you're sad or disappointed, when the clock tells us it's 3:00, the iPad will be put away. Will you want to play a game after that?

"Pretend the clock says it's 3:00 right now and I need to put the iPad away. What will you do? Will you say, *'No no no!'*? If you do, that's okay. I will still do my job and put the iPad away. Will you say, 'Okay, Mama'? If you do, I will still do my job and put the iPad away." Then, let your child pretend. Be playful, have fun. The more you can play with it, the less fraught it will feel for both of you when it actually happens.

This might seem silly or staged, but it really, really works, so I hope you will try this!

You can also encourage your child to play about the new limits while they aren't under pressure to comply. Here's what this might look like for a three-year-old who is used to having free access to the iPad, and now they don't. Sit down with your child and their favorite stuffed animal and together, explain the new routine to your child's doll. Then, let your child comfort the animal if they are sad or mad. Let your child take the role of adult and own the new routine. They can mentally rehearse new situations, explore their feelings about changes, and gain a sense of control and ownership over what is happening.

The bottom line is that screens aren't going anywhere, so we need to learn how to deal with them. Remember: The long-term goal is that scrolling a screen is not your child's default behavior. The goal is for your child to use screen time for intentional enjoyment.

Model your own awareness about your personal screen usage out loud. When you notice you've been on your phone/computer too much and it's affecting your mood, talk about it to your child. "I have been looking at my screen so much today, and now I feel cranky. I am going to put it away and go lie in the sun to feel better." You've modeled the problem and the solution.

SCREEN TIME DISCUSSION FOR OLDER KIDS

As your child grows up, involve them in the conversation about screen time habits. While it might sound counterintuitive, ask them how much screen time *they* think they need (for teens and tweens). Ask them what they feel is fair. Ask your teen or tween how you can support them instead of working against them. You are the grown-up, and you get to make the rules. But . . . a little compromise can go a long way. Children, at any age, want to feel seen and heard. They want the adults in their lives to understand how they feel, and there's no exception when it comes to screens. Try asking your older children:

- What feels like a good amount of screen time for you?
- When do you want your screen time to be?
- What feels fair to you?
- What do you wish you were allowed? Why?
- Tell me about what it's like with your friends. What devices are they using and when?
- Do you think that would work for you? Why or why not?
- How do you think screen time affects your mood, sleep, or schoolwork?
- What activities do you enjoy that don't involve screens?
- Do you ever wish there was a time of day without screens?
- What concerns do you have about screen time?
- If you were the adult in charge, what rules would you put in place?

By asking these questions, you're opening up a conversation that can lead to a more thoughtful discussion with your teen or tween. The goal is to foster a healthy relationship with technology while also maintaining your role as a parent in guiding and setting appropriate boundaries. They will likely still feel angry, frustrated, etc., and that's okay. Your job is to set the limit, and they are allowed to feel however they feel about it.

At best, screens entertain children, and children do not need to be entertained. Nor is it your role to entertain them. The more they learn to do it themselves, the better they will become at it. Is there a messy in-between when they are figuring out what to do instead of screens? Yes. Support them through it without fixing it.

Screen time limits will look different for all children and all families. There is no one-size-fits-all solution to screen time. Do your own research. Make decisions that feel best to you. And know that your child *can* play, and your role is to make space for play in their lives.

Keep the conversation open and ongoing. It is not your job to keep your child happy, it is your job to keep them safe and healthy and that includes screen usage. It is okay if your child disagrees with you. Stay respectful, listen to their opinions, but make your own decisions that align with your goals for your family. You are the strong and sturdy leader in your own home.

PART TWO

10

HOW TO SET UP YOUR HOME FOR INDEPENDENT PLAY

Your home environment has a much greater influence on your child's ability to play independently than you might realize. Creating a home environment that encourages self-directed exploration can significantly impact your child's ability and drive to play independently. It can also offer you some much-needed moments of peace!

Inspired by the Reggio Emilia Approach, I view a child's environment as a "third teacher" that can silently support their learning and play. When you set up your home in a way that does some of the work for you, you'll be setting the entire family up for success. This might sound overwhelming, but I assure you that organizing your home to promote independent play doesn't have to be expensive, fancy, or complicated. We are not looking for perfection here. There is nothing I like to see *less* than a well-meaning parent taking "play advice" to mean that they need to dive in head-first, overhaul everything, and buy all new play items. No! That is a first-class ticket to disappointment.

Instead, I want you to start with what you have at home right now. Let's look together and examine your kid's current play environment. You're doing a lot right already! I can help you make small consistent changes that will guide your child toward even more curiosity and exploration over time. You don't need to invest in pricey gadgets or special toys. Rather, I want to show you how to use what you have to create a play space that suits your family and your child.

The size or location of your home is irrelevant. What is important, though, is that you read this through the lens of your particular child's personality and developmental stage. Remember what you learned as you began to observe your child more intentionally, and think about those central family values we established earlier in the book. Keep those things at the top of your mind as you read this chapter.

Your Home Is Not a Social Media Post

A lot of people have come to me wanting to create a social-media-post-worthy playroom. They ooh and ahh over those pictures of gorgeous playrooms filled with wooden toys, closed-door cabinets, and neat-as-a-pin floors and tabletops. Sure, those images are beautiful, but does anyone actually play in those rooms?

Playrooms gained significant attention on social media in the late 2010s and early 2020s. The trend was driven by lifestyle influencers on Instagram showcasing elaborate rooms, followed by an increase in playroom-related content on Pinterest. I know this because I was one of those influencers, and many images of my own playroom went viral! The pandemic in 2020 further accelerated this trend. When every mom you knew was ordering food and medicine online in spring 2020, I was reminding them to add sidewalk chalk, paper, stickers, and indoor climbers to their list!

These days most of us are spending more time viewing other people's homes on social media than we are visiting with people in their homes. The perfectly curated rooms of all-wooden toys are certainly aspirational. But remember: The homes we view on TikTok are designed to sell us something. They present us with beautiful creamy rugs, brass touch-operated lamps, and faux shearling throws. They present these spotless spaces . . . while the rest of their stuff (and their children's plastic toys) are just off-screen. We can't see their real-life play areas. That's intentional. The more time we spend scrolling, the more our view of how homes *really* look gets skewed. I speak from experience.

Those playrooms may look beautiful online, but usually they are not functional. When I see a tall shelving unit outfitted with rope bins, I want to scream! Children cannot play there independently. They can't reach their toys, they don't know what's inside those beautiful containers, and it is nearly impossible for them to walk in and just start playing. Nope, they'll need help to pull down the items that they want, they can't expand their ideas by taking from other toys, and you can forget an independent cleanup time.

Instead of considering your child's play area as an aesthetic showroom for their toys, think about it as a container for their play experiences. I love that parents are thinking about play spaces, but I don't love the pressure or the perfectionism. Aesthetics are a great overlay if that's important to you, but what matters first is creating an intentional space that is reflective of your child's development and uniqueness, and also that fits in with your family's culture and the space you have in your home.

I am not saying that you can't have a beautiful home or playroom. You can. But it's equally, if not more important for your home to look like your kids live there. If you want your kids to play productively and spontaneously, then your home is going to look like a place where play happens. There might be toys in the living room (gasp!) and crayons and paper on the kitchen table. The cushions on your couch might be rumpled and your blankets will probably be used for forts. If your goal is a strictly aesthetic home, this is the wrong book for you—or at least the wrong chapter.

By providing a secure environment that reflects your child's personality and encourages exploration, you empower them to engage deeply in play. This approach nurtures their independence and enriches their creative and cognitive skills. Remember, the best play area is one that your child actually plays in. So, let go of the pressure to conform to trends, and embrace your child's play. A played-in home is messy. There's a little bit of marker on the table. There are some toys on the floor. It's proof of life, proof of learning, proof of playing.

Let's dive in to how you can make this happen in your home.

Personalizing the Play Area

The first question to ask yourself is: Where in your home will be most effective for both your child's play *and* your independence from your child's play? Grab a piece of paper, or note in the margin of this book, the top three places that you spend the majority of your time at home. For me, that would be the kitchen, my home office, and my primary bathroom (a girl's gotta have time to do her hair . . .). Yours might include a place where you work out, or maybe the laundry area of your home. Imagine those well-trafficked areas of your living space. How can you carve out a nook *there* for spontaneous play, so that your child can look to their environment instead of you for stimulation?

When my children were small, I spent a good portion of my days washing and folding the laundry. My youngest especially always followed me down to the basement laundry room and would inevitably start perusing my husband's nearby workbench and pawing through the bottles of detergent. Neither of those things were safe for a toddler! So I cleared the bottom shelves of detergents and put child locks on the workbench. In the space where the detergents used to sit, I put a few magnetic tiles, which are fantastic for sticking to the washing machine. I put a basket of old magazines, some child-friendly scissors, and a few of her favorite board books. I also put a small basket of rags for her to fold and socks for her to match. When she followed me down to deal with the laundry, she had stuff to do. She could fold like Mama or get busy with her toys. Either way, I was free to do my work while she did hers nearby.

Start to think about your own home in this way. What practical steps can you take to encourage your child's independence while also making your daily routine more manageable?

If you are lucky enough to have a dedicated playroom, you may be thinking that you shouldn't have to put toys in different areas of the house. Can't you just send your kids off to the playroom? Nice in theory, but you've probably already noticed that this doesn't work so well in practice. I've consulted with many families who have a designated playroom in the basement or on the top floor of the home, and they are puzzled when their children don't use it (especially the younger children). This actually makes perfect sense. If you watch a toddler at play, you'll notice that they sporadically and continually look to their grown-up—glancing up from time to time to check on where you are or wandering over to show you something. They are looking for emotional cues and reassurance. Your presence as they learn to play independently builds their confidence to explore their environment and follow their own curiosities. They don't necessarily want to play with you (you don't need to take over their play); they just want you to be easily accessible. You act as an anchor for them, even when you're not actually interacting with them.

When my husband and I bought our first house, my son was newly two years old, and I was pregnant with my daughter. I couldn't wait to set up a "real" playroom. As a former nursery school teacher and the daughter of a mom who provided my sisters and me with an open space to play in our childhood home, I was filled with ideas. I used tape on the floor to make parking spaces for my son's trike and ride-on toys. I outfitted the shelves with trucks and cars, and my father-in-law built us a custom shelf for our collection of wooden blocks. Every day, we'd trek down to the basement together for him to get playing . . . but the second I started up the stairs to the kitchen, there he was scampering up behind me.

It was fine. I saved the dishes and other housework for his naptime, and we made it work. I was determined to use the space I had created for him, so we kept going down there, and he kept following me back upstairs.

Then, my daughter was born. Forget saving housework for naptime. She was a newborn, so there was no set naptime. Meanwhile, my son was getting ready to drop his nap completely. My workload had tripled overnight, and I was overwhelmed. How could I wash the bottles, change all those diapers, and keep the house in order with two kids? This was harder than I thought it would be.

One day, my son wanted me to "see his trains in the basement" while my daughter needed changing and feeding. In a fit of frustration, I used my superhuman mom strength and pulled that bulky train table up the stairs all by myself. I set it right in the middle of our living room; my perfect decor and beautifully arranged furniture would have to be reshuffled for the time being. The kid needed his trains, and I needed to tend to my newborn.

All afternoon, my son played happily while I flitted back and forth between him, the baby, and everything else I needed to do in the main living area of the house. It was a good day. My husband came home that night, looked around, and said, "What's happening here?"

"I need to sterilize bottles, and he needs to play," I said. At first, my husband worried that the kids were "taking over" the house, and that's a common reaction. He wanted toys in the playroom and adult spaces in our main living area.

"Our house is starting to look like a preschool," he said.

Then the next evening, after we finished our supper, something miraculous happened. Usually, the moment he'd finished his meal, my son (understandably) got restless and wanted to leave the table. In the past, this signaled the end of dinner for my husband and me, too—whether we were done with our meals or not. After all, someone had to follow our son out of the kitchen and down to the playroom. But that day, rather than disrupting our quiet evening meal, my son simply climbed down from his chair when he was finished eating and started playing with his trains in the next room. My husband and I were able to sit at the table in the kitchen for much longer than we were used to, chatting (a real adult conversation!) and finishing our meals. My husband was thunderstruck (and frankly, so was I!). Once he realized the benefits of this new arrangement, my husband never again said a peep about the play spaces in our main living area. It was a game changer for our family.

I worked with a client a few years ago who was floored by the impact creating a small play area in her kitchen had on her family life. With a little bit of prodding from me, she reluctantly put a small table and chair and a basket of her child's favorite dinosaurs and cars in her kitchen. She had been constantly scolding her four-year-old to "stop climbing up on the kitchen counter" and stop pulling on her while she was preparing meals. She often relied on the iPad to keep him distracted during the busy afternoon hours. Suddenly, after the introduction of the kitchen play space, that dynamic completely shifted. Now she finds herself watching her son happily playing while she is busy with her new hobby: baking. She even started bringing her son in on the action, allowing her son to knead dough and mix his own concoctions on his little table.

"Wow, I can't believe how focused he is when he plays now," she said to me. "I'd never really seen him play independently because he always used to ask me to play with him. Now, he's so engaged, and I can really see the benefits for both of us. I'm watching him grow confident and independent while I'm getting to spend time on something I really love."

As my own family grew to three kids, our main floor play spaces expanded as well. Our small home had a formal dining room off the kitchen, and we never used it. We were a young family who certainly did not have the time or energy for formal entertaining of any sort. So, away went the dining room table and the cream-colored rug, and in came the block shelf, the play couches, and the rest of the well-loved items from our basement play space.

It was magical. The amount of daily playtime exploded exponentially, and it got more creative and expansive as well. It became easy for me to offer support with sibling interactions and fallen towers, while also doing my own work and dedicating time and attention to the things that were important to me. The play couches offered a comfy place for me to sit, when I wanted to, and observe them at play. These changes happened in steps, not all at once, and each step made our lives easier.

I can't believe we hadn't made this switch earlier. Learn from my mistakes. Use the basement for something else and put your "playroom" on your main floor. The benefits are worth the changes.

If You Have a Playroom

If you are lucky enough to have an actual dedicated playroom in your home, you have a great opportunity. A playroom doesn't have to be large or beautifully decorated, but it does have to be a spot where they have safe and unfettered access to their play materials. What matters is not the size or grandeur but value that is placed on it by the adults in their life.

What also matters is the condition of the playroom. The truth is—and I feel like I've said this so many times to clients—that the number one way to get kids to play in their playroom is to clean it. The second it is super clean, they are in there playing. They can't wait. And they're going to mess it up again! But the point is that if you really clean it, and it's really organized, they will want to go in there. Right now, as I write this in the kitchen, I'm avoiding my office because it's so messy and distracting. I can't get to what I need because there is so much clutter. Your children will feel the same way about a messy playroom, and play is, after all, your child's work.

I remember a client once saying to me that she couldn't understand why her daughter would play at the daycare in the gym she went to, but not at home. She said her daughter would run into that gym and start playing all by herself, never once mentioning that she needed help or wanted to watch a screen or didn't know what to do. At home, however, my client said her daughter would whine and complain that there was nothing to do.

"Our playroom is full of toys!" she said, shaking her head. "I don't get it."

I didn't get it, either . . . until I went over to her house and got a look at her playroom. Then it was obvious: a dollhouse tipped over onto a piled-high toy chest, blocks and puzzle pieces scattered on the floor, and big boxes of random items mixed together. There was little floor space. There were certainly a lot of toys in there, but they weren't accessible or organized. Many of us can likely relate to this scenario, because who wants to go in and spend the whole weekend cleaning a playroom?

But I promise you this: A clean playroom is a playroom that gets used. It's worth the work.

Which is not to say that it's easy to keep these spaces organized and tidy. The biggest culprit: too much stuff. It's hard to get rid of things because our children, and even we ourselves, have emotional attachments to toys and our child's creations, even when nobody uses them anymore. I'll talk more about how to curate the toys in your home in chapter 14, but what I can talk about here are some methods for organizing your playroom and making the things in it more accessible and play-ready.

Keep Toys at Kid Level

When my first child was about eight months old, I was up one night rocking him in his nursery as he recovered from croup. He wouldn't sleep if I put him down, and my anxiety over having a feverish coughing baby fueled my adrenaline. As the first light of dawn peeked through the windows of our apartment, my mind began to wander. I started to imagine a play space inside his bedroom instead of the random toys scattered around our apartment. The next morning, with lots of coffee in my system, I carefully placed him for a nap in the living room while I got to work in his room.

I took his DUPLO blocks out of the hard plastic case they came in and carefully set them right onto the low, open shelving unit in his room so that he could crawl over and take them down himself. I took his cars out of the zippered pouch we kept them in and I lined them up on the lowest shelf. I took his collection of stuffed animals and put them in a low open basket. I put a few favorite board books and his favorite lovey on a low, sturdy shelf.

As I arranged his toys, I thought about my years teaching preschool. Each year, as I set up my classroom, I would think about accessibility. I wanted the children in my care to feel that the classroom and materials belonged to them. I wanted to give them autonomy when they walked through the door. They didn't have to ask permission to use available materials. If, during the day, they needed a tissue to wipe their nose, I wanted them to be able to get a tissue themselves. If they felt thirsty, they could get their cup from their cubby and get a drink of water. They didn't have to ask me. I wanted the same feeling for toys in my son's room. In the words of my friend Susie Allison of Busy Toddler fame, "Play is the work of childhood and toys are the tools for their play."

Skip the Fancy Boxes and Bins

Some ideas for furnishings: Low and open shelving is the way to go. I like the look of gorgeous wooden cabinets with closed doors meant to stow toys out of sight, but they don't help children play. Children need to see their toys and be able to access them independently.

When possible, place items directly on the shelf or on a tray instead of in a bin. The tray makes it easy for your child to carry the materials to the floor or table. Inspired by Montessori education, trays can be used to help your child develop independence and organization. If a toy has too many parts for a tray or direct placement on the shelf, I recommend using a clear sturdy bin without a lid, so your child can see what's in it and get into it without help.

Engage Their Interests

Do they love animals? Set out some animal figurines, animal books, etc., on the play shelf. Do you have an outer space enthusiast? Encourage their curiosity with a few solar system books, a solar system puzzle, and a rocket ship. If you have a child who loves to sing, dance, and perform, include a basket of play silks and clips, and a pretend microphone.

Avoid Stacking

Nothing deters a child from play more than having to pull a game out from the bottom of a precariously stacked pile of games and puzzles. It is hard to find the one they want, hard to access it, and by the time they do, they've used up their attention span trying to get started. Choose one or two puzzles for the toy shelf and then put the rest of the puzzles into individual bags. Cut out the picture of the puzzle from the box and put that in the bag with the pieces for easy storage.

By the way, I never put games in the playroom because they are not for independent play. I keep them in the living room, put away. Then we can pull them out when playing a game with the family. While siblings can play a game together, typically that won't happen with an adult, and if siblings do want to play, they can go into another room.

Use the Right Furniture

A sturdy child-sized table makes a great workspace. If you don't have one, try subbing in a low coffee table. They are easy to find secondhand and hit at the perfect height for a preschooler or toddler. In a pinch, I have even used a bench meant for table seating as a work surface for young children. Get creative and use what you have easy access to.

Keep the tabletop clear. If your child uses this table for art, store an art trolley or rolling cart nearby with supplies, or use it for smaller toys or tabletop toys. I recommend pulling the table away from the wall and setting it up in the center of the room so it's ready for play from all sides. When they are finished, teach kids to get in the habit of clearing the space, which will be much easier if there are bins to put everything in. Think of this as resetting the space for the next session of independent play.

If you have the space, putting a couch or an adult-sized chair in your child's play area can be a game changer. It gives you a spot to do your own thing while you anchor your child in their play. As you've learned, the best way to get your kids in the habit of play is to hang out in their play space or make your spaces shared. Humans love proximity but you don't have to play with them. Read your own book silently, or watch them without joining. Get comfortable in their presence without being in charge of what they are doing. The chair or couch can act as a physical boundary to remind your child that you are nearby, but not available to play with them.

Pro Tip: If you need to be in the kitchen, the bathroom, or the baby's room, you can take one playroom bin or tray and bring it in there with you for your child. In essence, you are creating a mobile play pocket—like satellite offices for play—according to your own needs.

As you work on your home in this way, don't forget that it should not be difficult or intimidating. If you start to feel like creating an environment that supports your child's play requires a knack for interior design or a degree in early childhood education, take a step back and see where you can simplify. You don't need to buy new toys or invest in an entirely new playroom. Focus your efforts where they'll have the most impact by placing opportunities for play in the most used areas of your home. Whether it's magnetic tiles stuck to the fridge or a basket of small animals in the laundry room, strategic play pockets can transform the feel inside your home, and organized play spaces will help your children play easily without your intervention.

11

THE POWER
OF PLAY POCKETS

Many families don't have an extra room at home to use as a playroom and may feel that is a barrier to independent play. In smaller homes or homes without designated playrooms, parents may feel that they can't make a space for their children to play independently without messing up the main living spaces. If you have a playroom and your kids use it, that's great, but it's not a requirement. All you really need are play pockets.

Pockets of Play for Everyday

A play pocket is a nook for play in a room used for something else. You can set up play pockets throughout the house in areas where your child gravitates to playing naturally. These can be fixed or mobile. Play pockets allow your kids to play independently next to you, while you do the work you need to do. They open up your home to play areas not limited just to a playroom or a child's bedroom.

You can build these into wherever it's convenient. Place a beloved toy on the kitchen floor, set up a puzzle on the coffee table, or keep some crayons and paper on the kitchen counter. This approach encourages spontaneous play, making it easier for your child to engage no matter where they are in the house. It's a simple yet effective way to integrate play into their daily life. Low effort on your end, but very high reward. They'll love discovering an invitation to color at the counter while you make dinner.

If you have a basket of toys in the bathroom, you can be blowing out your hair, putting on your makeup, or taking a shower while your young child, whom you can't leave unattended, is sitting on the floor playing. Better to have them rolling toy cars or hammering pegs than ripping open a box of tampons or squirting the hand soap all over the floor. And you won't have to keep saying, "Don't do that!"

These play pockets can be in the areas where you most often need to do things, not just the kitchen and the bathroom but in the baby's room, in or just outside your home office, or in the family room, for when you want to read a book or have a conversation.

Look around your home for spaces where your child tends to hang out. Look for cubbies, corners, empty tables, or places where you could stow a small desk or a shelf. You could even get down on your hands and knees and look around your home from a child's point of view.

Where would your child want to play? Where will you be? Where might they play safely and within sight of you? Ask yourself, "Where does my child instinctively begin to play?" That's your clue to where you should set up for play. It doesn't have to be cute, it just has to be functional.

Maybe you could tuck a child-sized table into a corner of the kitchen, so your child can "work" while you make dinner. Can you stash a small cart of toys and a little rug next to the dining room table that you can easily put away if necessary? If these ideas don't match your values or the setup of your home, you can find what does. Get creative.

Once you've pinpointed a few options that you feel good about, try placing items of interest in those areas and see what happens. Don't lead your child to the play pocket. Let them discover it and use it on their terms. Kids want to feel ownership. Give it to them through play. With some trial and error, and your child's responses, you will likely discover the best play pockets.

For years, and especially during the COVID lockdowns, play pockets have been the second set of hands I needed to get my work done at home. When we all shifted to work from home, my youngest child was newly six years old. She loved to draw and make up elaborate stories as she created. Like most kids her age, waiting for Mom to get off a call so that she could ask a question or hang out was not her strong suit.

I felt frustrated that she kept interrupting and guilty for turning her away with a frantic, silent hand-waving motion. I told her multiple times not to interrupt, but she just couldn't help herself or remember. So, together, we came up with a solution. Anytime I was on a call, I pulled out a notepad of giant sticky notes and stuck them to the door of my office. Underneath it, I put sharpened pencils and markers. I drew a big stop sign on the top to remind her not to come in. Then, she would use the rest of the space to either draw a picture about what she wanted to tell me or to just free draw and write.

When I would get off my call, I would check the door and see what she'd created. I would reconnect with her by inviting her to tell me about the picture. It was such a helpful tool. She had a place to hold her ideas when she couldn't share them with me and

HOW CHILDREN MOVE DURING PLAY

Many parents worry that their child flits too quickly between activities, especially when they spend just a few minutes at the art table before bouncing to blocks, or fiddle with play dough briefly, then wander over to the dollhouse. There's a common misconception that a focused child will stay with one activity for a long time.

The truth is that young children naturally move from activity to activity. They might spend a little bit of time on play dough, a little bit of time building with blocks, then they might come back to the play dough, then wander over to look at a board book, then rock their stuffed animal, then go back to the board book. That's how young children play. Here is a diagram that shows typical preschool movement around a classroom or playroom:

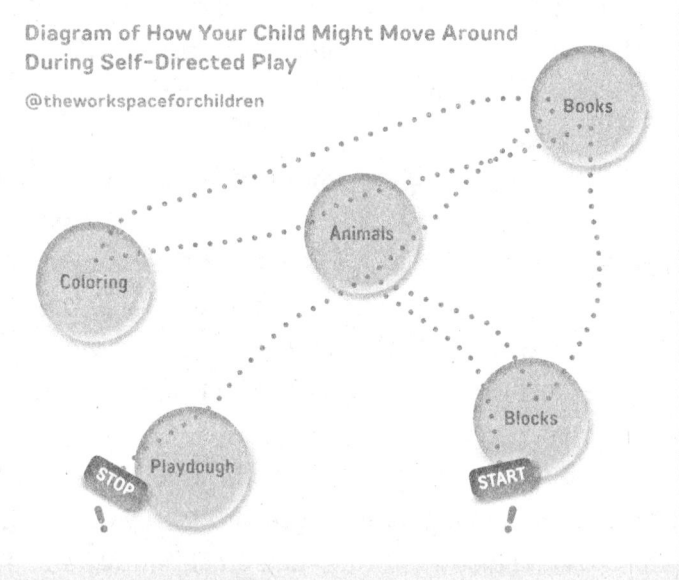

Diagram of How Your Child Might Move Around During Self-Directed Play

@theworkspaceforchildren

If you have multiple play pockets set up around your home, your child is already equipped to move from play area to play area and idea to idea without you having to do anything. When kids have this opportunity to flit around the play area, they can move right into that play brain space, and suddenly, they're not bored anymore. The ideas start coming and evolving, and *voilà!* They are playing. As you design play pockets in different spaces, keep this natural tendency to "browse" play areas in mind.

a visual reminder not to open my door. I grew to love seeing her little socked feet under the door when I was working and even more, I cherished the pictures and her invented spelling.

I helped a client with two little boys, four and six, curate a small collection of sidewalk chalk, mallets, buckets, and other toys on her back patio. At first, she was reluctant to designate another area where she'd have to clean up kid messes, but she agreed to try it. Her boys immediately started playing out there. She and her husband ended up sitting together on the patio with them while they played, having a beer, and enjoying the night. Before, she told me they could barely have a conversation because the kids were arguing or needing things, but once they had a back patio play pocket, that all changed.

Incorporating pockets of play in your home is powerful. People start to notice the impact that play has on their families almost immediately. The more your children start playing independently, the more play will become a part of your family's culture, and everything becomes easier. You are entertaining them less and have the ability to be a more present parent. Children feel that, and their behavior improves. Maybe these exact scenarios won't work for you, but let them inspire you to look at your home in a new way.

Play pockets will need your attention from time to time. Take a few moments a couple of times per week and tend to them. Like a garden, play pockets need to be cultivated, not left to grow wild. Tidy up, remove anything that's not being used, and add a little something here and there. If you actively nurture the space, your child will thrive within it.

Equipping a Play Pocket

Once you've decided on where your child's play pockets will be in your home, it is time to decide what to put there! This can be both exciting and a bit daunting, so I am going to help you outfit your play pockets with ease. Take the ideas that sound easy or fun to implement, and that will work best for you, and let the rest go for now. Remember, this should feel helpful, and if you start to feel overwhelmed, only choose one or two areas to work on.

In the Kitchen

The kitchen is the hub of family life. When I work with clients who have the space, I always encourage them to take their play kitchen out of the playroom and put it in the real kitchen. I've never had anyone put it back. Why? Kids love to mimic what they see. Are you busy cooking? So are they. You're cleaning your kitchen? Boom. Now they're busy cleaning their kitchen. Not only are they learning practical life skills, but they are busy playing while you're getting things done.

As your children grow from toddlers to preschoolers, adapt

that play kitchen. Take away some of the plastic fruits and vegetables and add more open-ended things like bowls, whisks, and small ceramic dishes. IKEA and the dollar store are great places to source these materials. As your child's interests and abilities grow, encourage them by giving them more grown-up and realistic materials. Eventually, you can start to incorporate real cooking tools like a paring knife and cutting board. Add one of those inexpensive pads of paper with checkboxes, for children to "take orders" or write recipes. Kids love this and it elevates the play kitchen just when they may be getting bored of it.

If you don't have space in your real kitchen for a play kitchen, that's okay. There are lots of other ways to get creative. Try clearing out one drawer that your child can access and fill it with toys that they love or kitchen items they can use. Flip a milk crate, throw a towel over it, and you'll have a space for pretend right at your feet. You can even use the milk crate to store their toys if you can't spare a drawer.

One of my favorite ways to incorporate play in the everyday is with a child-sized table and chairs. Instead of leaving it unused in their bedroom, set it in your kitchen or living room. You can put simple items on this table that reflect your child's interest, but rather than calling their attention to it, simply put something out there, such as a puzzle, and wait to see if your child approaches and uses it. Let them find it. I bet you'll turn around from the kitchen sink and see them puzzling away!

In the Bathroom

When I think back to the bathroom my kids used in their younger years, the one where we gave nightly baths, taught them how to brush their teeth, picked damp towels off the floor and returned them to their hooks, and held their hair back when they were sick,

I kind of miss it. It's pretty amazing when you realize that your child's bathroom is where you teach them skills they'll use daily for their entire lifetime. Let's get that bathroom space working for you and not against you.

When my kids were small and I would be doing my own get-ready routine, or tending to one child while the other waited, I did something that made some people stare strangely at me and others exclaim, "Great idea!" I cleared out one of the shelves under the sink and instead of extra toothpaste and toilet paper, I lined up the children's cars and toys. The extra toiletries found a new home in the hall closet, and I transformed the bathroom space into their play area. This minimized whining and made waiting their turn for teeth brushing or bathing less of a daily battle.

I'm sure you've seen the advice of keeping a basket of books in the bathroom when potty training. This is like that, but for waiting. Waiting is hard for kids. Make it easier on them and you both win.

In Your Child's Bedroom

Should you keep toys in your child's bedroom? There are lots of sides to this debate, with sleep experts weighing in all over social media. There is no right or wrong answer. But I've found that bedrooms can be an ideal place for at least *some* toys—for example, an older sibling's special toys that they don't want little siblings to break. (Often when a new baby arrives, big siblings lose some autonomy. Allowing your older child to have a space that can remain untouched by the new sibling does everyone good.)

If you decide to keep toys in your child's bedroom, try this: Get down to their eye level and take a look around. Does their room feel like a true reflection of who they are, or is it a catchall for toys, clothes, books, and things that don't really have a good home? Does their room feel comfortable and usable?

Think back to what you learned about your child when you began observing them more closely. Your child will thrive in a space that is both clean and reflective of who they are. Step by step, at a pace that works for you, you can begin adjusting your child's room so it's more pleasant to be in and easier to use.

I had a client whose six-year-old daughter loved small-world play. She had a dollhouse filled with furniture, a set of magnetic tiles, and wooden blocks for making enclosures and homes for her little people. She kept some art materials for drawing and cutting decorations to add to her creations. There were crafting kits, her art, and books all mixed together in a hodgepodge of play. It was very creative and totally reflective of this girl's personality.

Her mom reached out to me, exasperated by the chaos in her daughter's room. She said it felt like a "land mine" when she wanted to tuck her daughter in. She could barely get to the dresser to put away her daughter's clean clothes, and vacuuming felt impossible. Her daughter's creative play, once a source of pride, was becoming a daily battle between Mom and daughter, and they needed help.

I particularly enjoyed partnering with this client because she had a deep appreciation for her daughter's play personality. She saw the value in leaning into her child's passions. She also understood that it was important to have clear boundaries around the cleanliness and functionality of the child's room. Here's what we came up with.

First, she told her daughter how much she valued her play. She took photographs of some of the creative setups and playscapes her daughter had created and hung them on the walls. Then, she put some boundaries in place.

THE MAGIC OF A PLAY POUCH

Keep a small bag filled with portable play items like mini figurines, crayons, paper, sticky notes, and stickers. Mini magnetic toys are always a winner here. This can be a life-saver when you have to drag your child on endless errands, but you don't want them on a screen. You can easily grab this play pouch when you're heading out. (We kept one in the diaper bag and one in the car.) It's perfect for those moments when you're waiting in the pickup line, sitting at a restaurant, or watching an older sibling's sports practice.

Physical boundaries are a great way to keep the mess in one spot. You can make a physical boundary with something as simple as painter's tape or a rug. In this case, we used a large low coffee table that the client had in another room in her home. She cleaned up her daughter's shelf and removed all the little bits of trash or things that belonged elsewhere.

Then, she arranged her child's materials on the shelf with a clear place for each category—people, animals, vehicles, blocks. We used clear acrylic bins so that the child had a good visual of what went where and what she had on hand for play. Remember, toys that are put in opaque bins can mean out of sight, out of mind. The low table went in front of the shelf and that's where her dollhouse lived, leaving lots of room for expansion around.

The craft kits went into a cabinet in their kitchen where they were more likely to get used. Old artwork was sorted in a keep or recycle pile. Mom explained to her daughter that if she kept her small worlds on the table, Mom wouldn't touch them when she needed to vacuum or put away laundry. She could create as much as she wanted as long as it stayed on the table. If she wanted to expand beyond the table, that was fine, but it needed to be cleaned up within a day or two.

Her daughter loved her new play space and, for the most part, was able to stay within the boundary of the table. Mom felt great that she could support her daughter's storytelling, spatial thinking, and emotional processing while also keeping a clean and manageable space in her daughter's room. You don't have to sacrifice their creativity or your sanity.

Play pockets truly are at the heart of independent play because they make play so easy for your child and take so little effort on your part. I hope you'll embrace and institute this idea in your home. It really can be the solution to getting your kids playing right away.

12

READY, SET, PLAY!

t's time to play. Your child already plays, of course, and you've probably already tried a lot of ideas in this book that are working for you. In this chapter, I want to help you get them playing longer, with more productive periods of independent play, by setting up simple ways for them to get more invested in their play. You are going to step back and watch them take over while getting some much-needed time back for yourself. If you've been waiting and reading and thinking all of this, it's time to put these principles into action.

Some children will need more support than others, and that's okay. You're going to meet them where they are and start with the simple act of scheduling the time for them to play, just like you would schedule any other activity.

Scheduling Unstructured Play

We often schedule lessons, tutoring, and social events, so why not schedule play? Take a look at your family's weekly schedule and carve out dedicated time for play. It's just as important, if not more important, than structured activities. Research supports this—a 2014 study of six- and seven-year-olds showed that the kids with more unstructured time were better at tasks where they had to put things in categories and make decisions without help.

By committing to specific times for play, you're sending a message to your child that unstructured play is important. The more they practice playing, the better they'll get at playing independently. When you treat playtime with the same importance as other scheduled activities, their play will grow exponentially. If your child was great at soccer, and you went all in on soccer, they'd get better and better. They would receive positive feedback, their success would feel good to them, and they would want to work harder at it. When you schedule the time for play like you would for soccer, you are giving your child the advantage of investing in their own ideas and follow-through skills.

Finding the time for play isn't easy for all families. Even if scheduled unstructured time only happens on the weekends, it can still give your child the space they need to learn to play independently. When children play at home, they develop strong skills that they take back into the classroom, onto the soccer field, and into the world.

Play Prompts

A play prompt is a simple, open-ended invitation for your child to play. It's particularly useful for children who are resistant to exploring on their own, or who don't know how to get started. They prompt your child by sparking their imagination without your intervention. Play prompts can build play confidence in your child as they are learning to come up with their own ideas. It can also be useful on those "But I'm bored!" days. You may find that the better your child gets at independent play, the less you will utilize play prompts, but it's always nice to have them available when you need them.

Simple play prompts can be the cement that paves the way for a restless child to go from frazzled to focused, productive, independent play. Simple play prompts can also support a child who is figuring something out through play. A thought-out, open-ended prompt can boost your child to their next level of play, wherever they are on the independent play spectrum.

A play prompt is not a complicated project requiring purchases and supervision. Skip the elaborate crafts. Instead, use familiar items you already have and keep things simple. When parents overcomplicate play prompts, resentment and burnout follow, especially when children spend less time playing than you spent setting up.

Another trap that well-meaning parents fall into with the play prompt is putting themselves in the role of director instead of observer. Rather than "This is what we're making today," try leaving the prompt out in a prominent spot in your home or sitting and sharing a snack together while your child gets started. One of the best parts about play is that your child gets to be in charge.

It's not that you can't intentionally do projects with your kids. If you love crafting, building, or baking together, that is a fantastic way to connect. But those projects are not play prompts. They are entirely separate. A good play prompt sets the stage for play without directing the play. It's not something you teach them how to do. It takes advantage of what you know about your child and how they play, but it doesn't dictate the play. It just sets the stage for the play.

So what does a play prompt look like? If you were to look around inside a child-led preschool program, you would see some examples of what I'm calling a play prompt. For instance, you might see a low table with lumps of play dough and a few tools or interesting items to explore with the dough. You might see a water table with objects floating in it.

In the fall, teachers might set out pumpkins with markers and tools for exploration. They'll observe the children's natural interests and engage with their ideas, following the children's lead rather than directing the activity. The teacher is not saying, "Here's what we're going to do at the water table today—we will work on pouring," or "Today we are learning how to draw portraits of this pumpkin. Start with a circle, then make a line here . . ." The play areas and tools are for children to do what they find interesting and to satisfy their curiosity.

At home, maybe you'll gather some fall leaves and scatter them on a table with paper and crayons. You might do one leaf rubbing, or put a cut leaf next to some child-safe scissors, just so they can see what is possible. Then you step back and see what they will do.

You aren't sitting your kids down and saying, "Today after school we are going to do leaf rubbings. Here is how to do it." I'm not saying you can't do this—sometimes projects are fun, and children enjoy learning how to do new things from an adult. Your child might ask how you made the leaf rubbing, in which case you can support them in figuring it out, and then, you can step back and let them experiment with it.

A play prompt, as opposed to a project, is an invitation to your child to come over and do what *they* want to do. Your child might draw the pumpkin, or draw on the pumpkin, or draw something else. They might make a leaf rubbing, or trace the leaves, or make a leaf collage, or ignore the leaves completely. It doesn't matter what they do. What matters is that they are thinking of what to do on their own.

One time we found an old papery wasp nest. I put it out on a blanket with tweezers and a magnifying glass, and some paper and pencils to write and draw. What I didn't do was sit them down and say, "Let's learn about wasp's nests today." I did stay nearby to answer questions and reflect their play, but I didn't quiz them like, "What are the parts of the wasp's nest?" I let them make their own hypotheses and ask their own questions, and gave them the tools to answer those questions themselves. Later, they asked to go to the library to find some books about wasps, so we did.

Play prompts are an extra set of hands. The opportunities are there, but it's up to the child to decide whether and how to engage with the materials or not. Either way, the stakes are low for you because it took you very little time to set up the prompt.

Open-Ended Versus Closed-Ended

One of the qualities that makes play prompts so effective for independent play is that they are open-ended, meaning the material doesn't dictate the play, like a project with a beginning and an ending does. I had a client, a couple with a three-year-old named

Mia. The parents were frustrated because Mia couldn't play independently for more than a few minutes, constantly demanding their attention. Before we got into the details about supporting independent play, I asked to look at Mia's toys.

After observing Mia's play area, I noticed most of her toys had a specific way to use them. She had puzzles, games with set rules, and electronic toys that did the same thing each time you pressed a button. She also had shape sorters where each shape only fit in one spot, and play dough with mats directing her how to make letter shapes.

While these toys can be fun and teach certain skills, it's like the toy is telling the child, "This is how you play with me," instead of letting the child decide. Having only closed-ended toys also meant that Mia needed her grown-ups to intervene when she completed a task. For example, she needed them to open the shape sorter and take all the shapes out when she had dropped them in. She couldn't play independently, even when she was in a flow, so these toys didn't work well as play prompts.

I wanted to give Mia and her grown-ups a quick and easy win to help them see more independent play right away, so I suggested introducing some open-ended play prompts to Mia to allow her to lead her own play without needing adult support. Rather than have them purchase new toys, I suggested they open up the materials they already had.

To do this, I suggested that they take the shapes out of the sorter and instead, put them in a basket with a few small people figurines. That's a play prompt.

I showed them that they could remove the play dough mat that directed how to use the dough, and instead, knowing she loved animals, add small animals to a lump of dough so that she could pretend anything she wanted. That's a play prompt.

Instead of coloring books with pre-drawn pictures, I suggested an extra-large sheet of paper taped to the table with a few crayons and stickers. Another play prompt.

The change wasn't immediate, but over a few weeks, her moms noticed improvement. Mia started playing independently for longer periods, often up to twenty to thirty minutes at a time. She could find materials they set out on a table, and she would proceed to color, create with play dough, work on a puzzle, then go back to play dough. The open-ended prompts helped because they didn't dictate a "right" way to play. Mia could discover them and play however she wanted, which kept her interested longer.

Her moms were thrilled that they could complete small tasks while Mia played nearby. They also noticed Mia seemed more engaged and creative in her play. While not a miracle solution, using open-ended play prompts helped foster Mia's independence and creativity, giving her moms some much-needed breathing room.

Barriers to Entry

Toys that require preparation too difficult for young children can quickly become barriers to independent play. Imagine a big box filled with sealed jars of play dough and a lot of tools, with a snap-on lid. This might be how you store your play dough, but it's not a play prompt. There are too many things the child can't do themselves before they can start playing. Play dough is tough for small hands to pull out of the jar. But you can make a play prompt out of this play dough box by taking out and strategically placing selected items appropriate for the child.

Maybe you take out three play dough colors, removing the dough from the jars and mounding it on the table, along with one or two tools and some small favorite toys. Because you've taken away the hard parts of getting ready to play, they can just start playing. They don't have to fiddle with the tools or use their energy to dig out the color they want or figure out how to open the thing. This is frustrating. They have to ask for help. Then you tell them they have to wait a minute because you're in the middle of something, and they start whining, and then you get annoyed, and they start arguing, and by then, they've forgotten all about the play dough.

Those few quick preparatory steps make the difference between a chaotic, frustrating experience and a smooth, relaxing experience for both you and your child. We can all do things better when the environment is calm and what we need to do is easy.

Think about going to a big supermarket. As you enter, the lights are buzzing, it's crowded, music is blaring, your child starts whining, and there are so many choices. You abandon your list and start throwing things in your cart without really paying attention because you're so distracted. You get to the register and what you have suddenly seems so random. Then you get home, and you still can't figure out what to make for dinner. You are overstimulated and tired, and you order in.

Compare that to the experience of going into a tiny well-curated food market where they have a few prepared foods you already know you like, they cater to your dietary restrictions, and they've placed the foods you love on the shelf right where you can easily reach them. It's quiet in there and such an enjoyable experience. When you get home, you feel calm and inspired, and you are able to use what you bought to prepare an amazing meal.

This is the difference between a chaotic play area overflowing with toys, and simple play prompts in strategic play pockets around your home for your kids to play in easily.

Play Prompt Inspiration

Setting up play prompts is similar to how we make better choices with food. Imagine feeling hungry and irritable, staring into a crowded pantry. You might grab crackers and your child's leftover gummy bears, leaving you unsatisfied. But if someone set out fresh apple slices, cheese and crackers, and water, you'd remember how good it feels to have nourishing options readily available.

The same principle applies to play prompts. When we thoughtfully prepare the environment for play, we set our children up for success.

Here are some examples.

Let's say you have a basket of cars and a basket of blocks in the living room. A play prompt might be to clear off your coffee table, line up six blocks, put a car on top, and put the basket of blocks and cars next to it. That's a play prompt. It's low effort and it's open-ended, allowing your child to create a game out of it, of their own choosing. There is no pre-arranged beginning or end, just an opportunity to play.

Maybe you will put out puzzle pieces and fit a few of the pieces together, strewing the rest of the pieces out over the table—just enough to get them interested.

Maybe you set out a couple of pre-peeled stickers next to paper, with some markers.

Take your child's dollhouse off the shelf and put it on the kitchen floor with a few people and cars next to it. It's just enough to get started without directing a play scenario. They won't have to pull the dollhouse down themselves, and they might rediscover a forgotten toy. They can begin playing without sorting through everything first.

In fact, there are likely many toys your child hasn't thought about for a while. A fun way to set up a play prompt is to find those toys gathering dust in the playroom—those magnetic tiles they begged for? The Paw Patrol pup tower that is tipped over on its side under a pile of costumes? Or yes, that expensive dollhouse?

Choose one of them and set it up in an unexpected place, out of the playroom, such as the coffee table or the kitchen table. Grab yourself some coffee, sit back, and watch the magic happen when your child rediscovers that toy, out of context, and it seems new again. Your child will be playing in an instant.

This works because if your playroom is full of toys, your children are probably overwhelmed by choices and haven't actually played with many of the toys for a long time. This can be a good method for deciding whether to keep or give away a toy. When cleaning up the playroom, pick one thing, and set that up on the kitchen table as an experiment. If nobody's interested, then maybe that's a sign that it's time for that toy to go. If it sparks play, then it's a keeper.

Many two- and three-year-old kids are interested in large vehicles like construction equipment. Developmentally, they are exploring how things work and move. When my son was a toddler, he loved garbage trucks. I knew the garbage truck came on Tuesdays and Thursdays, so on those days, I put a little stool by the front window, along with some board books about garbage trucks and a few toy trucks.

It took me about two minutes to set up. Instead of waiting with him to see when the garbage truck is coming and then controlling the experience by saying, "Here it comes, let's go outside and see it" (and spending thirty minutes standing there), I set up a play prompt so he could have his own experience. I said, "Hey, the garbage truck is coming soon. I'm going to go wash dishes while you sit here and watch it. I wonder who the people on the garbage truck will be today!"

My son used to sit at that window for thirty minutes twice a week, while looking at his books and playing with his own trucks, then watching as the garbage truck arrived and emptied the garbage, then replaying the experience with his toy trucks, processing what he witnessed. When he got older, the board books were replaced by pencils and paper on a clipboard so that he could draw or create stories about what he observed.

When it comes to play prompts, remember that it's okay if your child doesn't use the play prompt and plays in another way. Resist the urge to say, "Hey, look what I set up for you! You can do X, Y, and Z with this!" Your child will be more engaged and build more play confidence if you just stand back and allow them to come to it on their own. Play prompts are meant to spark engagement and exploration for your child. Keep it simple so you aren't more invested in the prompt than they are.

13

ART AS PLAY

Drawing, coloring, painting, collage—all these forms of art come naturally to most children. In my mind and in my set-ups, art is play. Art prompts are essentially play prompts. They can be easy to set up and result in long periods of independent play. A roll of paper or a few sheets spread out on a table, a few crayons or markers or some washable paint, a few lumps of colored clay or collage materials and glue—the possibilities are virtually endless.

While art supplies are a category all their own, they can hold just as much play potential as any toy. A simple set of crayons and paper can captivate your toddler alongside your teenager. All children can benefit from making and creating art in their own way, whether that means they spend an hour carefully crafting tiny, detailed worlds or they quickly create bold sweeping marks across their page—both approaches are valuable.

When young children draw, paint, or sculpt, they discover how different materials feel and work. Working with various art supplies helps them develop fine motor skills that they'll need to write and tie their shoes. Art is not just an "extra" for the "creative" kids. All children benefit immensely from repeated experiences to create.

What makes art supplies so special is that they meet each child exactly where they are, growing alongside them as their interests and abilities develop. Your toddler might start by making marks on paper and experiencing the sensation with their body, while your older child uses the same materials to draw and write an elaborate story. Without a right or wrong way to create and no predetermined outcome, your child is free to make the supplies into whatever they need them to be.

When I was a child, my mom set up an art table in our kitchen. It was something unique to our family. I didn't know anyone else as lucky as we were to be able to create every day. It was a simple setup with a sturdy child-sized table and chairs, and a set of drawers filled with stickers, markers, tape, scissors, and paper. My siblings and I colored and stickered (and bickered) while she cooked dinner or prepared lunch for us. Many of my favorite childhood memories take place seated around that art table.

Naturally, when I had my own children, I wanted to re-create the feeling of my childhood art table. Our home was much smaller than the home I grew up in, so I had to get creative. One day, during my son's naptime, when I was pregnant with my daughter and probably should have been napping myself, I cleared out all of the pots and pans from the cabinet and put art supplies in there instead. The cabinet had drawers inside, and it was at child height, just perfect for art supplies!

Remember how I told you my husband was surprised by the train table in the kitchen? Well, he was even more shocked when he opened the cabinet to pull out a pot and found a carefully curated supply of markers, paper, and stickers, instead. I shoved the pots into the uppermost cabinet, letting them clatter and nest however they fell. But . . . I had my priorities in order. I knew that giving my son access to sturdy supplies would encourage him to create and play.

That first art cabinet was lean, reflecting my two-year-old son's interests and abilities. There was a small pile of paper, washable markers, and stickers. I added only enough stickers and paper that if he used them all in one sitting, I would be okay with it. In front of the cabinet, I put a small table for him to work at. He loved it! Twos crave independence, and he felt so big and important having his own cabinet of supplies for his work. I put a small trash can underneath the table so that he could clean up independently, and that was a hit, as well. When we confidently allow children appropriate responsibility and autonomy, they almost always rise to the expectation. As he grew in ability and maturity, we added scissors, tape, and cardboard. His confidence exploded, and he began to regard himself as a kid who was great at making things.

When my daughter was a toddler, she, of course, became very interested in the art cabinet. Her toddler development drove her to seek cause-and-effect relationships, and she loved to open and close the cabinet doors, satisfied by both the predictable nature of the door and the scream that would erupt from her brother when he was sure she'd demolish the whole thing.

But I had a problem. I wanted my daughter to have the same opportunity that my son had, yet they were at very different developmental levels and needed different materials. I did not want to interrupt the hours of independent play the art cabinet was providing for my son (and me).

So, what did I do? I put a child lock on the art cabinet and taught my four-year-old how to open it. Then, I put a few simple supplies out on the table for my toddler. He took great pride in being responsible about closing up his big kid supplies when not in use, and she was so happy to be in on the creating at the table.

Was it perfect? No way. Did she end up coloring on the wall and her face a few times? You betcha. But everything was washable, and I was rooted in my core parenting value that their play was their work. This helped me see that it wasn't a big deal.

Creating an Art Space

If you want your children to be able to engage with art without you having to set everything up, you can create an independent art space in your home—essentially, an art play pocket. Here are some ideas:

- Use a rolling cart that can be put away when not in use.

- Have a sturdy and consistent workspace that you don't mind getting marked up.

- Keep your supplies lean and organized. Start with only three or four materials and build as your child matures.

- Add a garbage can to encourage independent cleanup.

As your children grow and their interests develop, expand the materials available to them. The tools may stay the same, but your child will develop and grow to use basic materials in increasingly advanced ways. Less is more when it comes to self-serve supplies.

For each of my three children, the art cabinet meant something different. My oldest, cerebral in nature, used the materials in the art cabinet as tools for investigation. He measured, drew exact models of airplanes, and experimented with weight and balance in his sculptures.

My middle daughter, an artist at heart, used the art cabinet to fulfill her need for color and design. She spent hours as a child mixing shades of paint to achieve a single color that she saw in nature. She collaged and created massive colorful murals in our kitchen.

My youngest, a storyteller, used the art cabinet to make props to support her imaginative play. She used scissors to clip out tiny capes for her stuffed mice, colored tape to construct outfits for her stuffed animals, and a whole lot of paper to create elaborate scripts for her pretend games. Basic, sturdy materials and free access will empower your children to direct their own creativity.

As they start to use the art space, take time to observe your children as they set up, work, and clean up. Be curious about their experiences, and use your observations to continue to reinvent the space to match their ages, stages, development, and interests.

How to Respond to Your Child's Artwork

Art is a kind of play children often like to share with their adults after playtime. They love to show you what they drew, painted, or sculpted, and are excited to get your reaction. Yet, this can be tricky. Let's take an aside for a moment to talk about a common situation that happens when parents are supporting their child's play or connecting afterward.

You know that moment when your child proudly shows you their drawing and you have no clue what it is? They are beaming at you with expectation and you say, ". . . That's beautiful, honey!"

WHEN PARENTS WANT TO JOIN IN ON ART PROJECTS

Art is an area where parents overthink, direct, or even join in, in ways that can turn children away from this kind of work. A lot of parents like to draw and color. It's fun and relaxing, and they rarely have the opportunity. They dive into the art prompt, creating adult-level work. They want to use the opportunity to teach their child to draw and create.

Inadvertently, this can pose a problem for young children. When you start drawing, your child compares their work to yours. They may feel intimidated or frustrated that they can't draw something as well as you did. Or, they might see that you did it so well that they should just let you draw, unintentionally discouraging independent exploration and reducing their confidence. Children can become overly focused on replicating work, rather than developing their own ideas. They defer to adults for "better" drawings, shifting focus from the process of creation to achieving a perfect product.

When mentoring student teachers in my classroom, one of my key instructions was always this: "When you're working with the children, please avoid drawing for them or creating your own artwork. Your role is to support their exploration of the materials—you can mirror their actions, but avoid making your own independent creations. This helps prevent children from comparing their work to yours and keeps the focus on them."

Then you inwardly panic that they'll realize that you have no idea what they drew.

Let's think about how we respond to our children's artwork. Do you offer them a conversation starter or a conversation ender?

Does your child create from within for herself, or does he scribble a few lines and look for praise? Just like when your child is playing with toys, we want to redirect the conversation back to our child's ideas and opinions, not our own.

I've spent a lot of time over the years observing children making art (clay, paint, drawing, etc.). I love to watch and listen, to be a very quiet presence, only interacting if invited, and even then, only reflecting back their own words and mannerisms to them. I really respect their process. I don't want to take away from it by distracting them with my own adult notions. When you are a very still presence, you can learn so much about the inner workings of a child's mind as they create art.

Sadly, there have been so many times when a child is deep in the process, and I will see an adult (teacher or parent) with the best of intentions squash the whole thing in one fell swoop. They'll ask, "What are you making?" or they might interject about how beautiful the creation is.

Now, I know that seems so innocent, and many people think that's what they are supposed to be doing in order to engage with and encourage a child. But I want you to stop for a moment. Think about when you are cooking. You are using all of your senses to read the recipe, measure, taste, smell the aromas. Would you not find it distracting if someone popped up on your countertop and started asking you questions about the final outcome? What if they wanted to talk about the recipe and micromanage how you are following it? What if they thought you were making meatloaf when really, you were making soup? How annoying would that be? Would you feel the relaxing enjoyment that you might otherwise derive from making your favorite soup?

It's the same thing for our children when they are creating. Sometimes, our well-intentioned input takes the joy out of creating and becomes about us and not them. They have their entire

181

lives ahead of them to be judged, both by themselves and others. Right now, while they are still young and creating for the pure joy of creating, let's really try to honor that.

Here's how:

- **Be a quiet presence.** Observe closely and try not to comment unless invited by the child.

- **Use reflective language.** When your child says, "I'm making a picture of Mommy," just repeat that back. "Oh, you are making a picture of Mommy." Resist the urge to squeal and gush and change the course of things.

- **Allow your child the repeated use of sturdy, simple materials.** Gaining mastery over basic materials (crayons, paper, scissors) gives them the opportunity to express themselves, problem-solve, and grow over time. You will be amazed at what they come up with when the materials are basic and open-ended.

- **Honor the process.** Making art with children is about exactly that: the making. The process. The creating, not the creation. Be as in tune, if not more in tune, with the creative problem-solving process as you are with valuing the final outcome.

- **Have fun and create often.**

Let's take a look at some examples.

Conversation One:

Child: *Mommy, look at my drawing!*
Mom: *Wow! That's so pretty. Is it a person?*

Child (somewhat dejectedly): *Um, no, it's a big scary monster.*
Mom: *Oh . . . right! Of course it is.*

Conversation Two:

Child: *Mommy! Look at my drawing.*
Mom: *I see your drawing! You used bright blue and it looks like you made some big motions with your arms to draw those lines.*
Child (excitedly): *Yeah, because it's a big monster and I had to draw how strong he is.*
Mom: *It is a big, strong, blue monster! I wonder why you chose blue?*
Child: *The blue is because he hides in the sky when he is sneaking up on people.*
Mom: *Sneaking up on people? That sounds interesting.*
Child: *Yes . . . he sneaks up on people and then he yells Rawr!!!*
Mom: *He yells Rawr? That sounds really scary.*

Can you see the difference in these two conversations? In the first conversation, the child is excited to share and then he seems unsure how. The second conversation is child-led and the adult supports the child in confidently sharing her work and ideas. Still not sure how to do this? I got you:

- **Instead of guessing what your child made,** notice something about the picture. "Tell me about that red part."

- **Comment on the color.** Oh! You chose yellow to make those marks.

- **Comment on lines and shapes.** You used lines that zigzag and some dots in your work.

What about when they are frustrated or looking for help? It's tempting for us as parents to tell our kids, "No, that looks great!" or "It's not a big deal!" or "Let me show you how." But the truth is, kids just want us to understand how they are feeling inside. Give them the words that match their feelings and you'll see them work through their frustrations much more productively.

Try these three phrases to support your kids through their frustration and get them back to creating.

- "That didn't come out the way you wanted it to."

- "You're wishing it looked different. I see that."

- "I remember when I was learning to draw. It was tricky for me, too."

When you approach the art this way, you can really examine their picture together without assuming anything.

If Your Child Doesn't Like Art

People often message me about their child who "doesn't like art." Saying your child "doesn't like art" is like saying your child "doesn't like to play," so why would a child say they don't like playing with crayons or paint or clay? I immediately begin to wonder if they've only been introduced to structured arts and crafts.

Young children don't need to make cutesy crafts or be taught how to draw certain things with certain techniques. Interested children can benefit from drawing instruction when they are older, but toddlers and preschoolers are not ready for structured outcomes.

Structured art and crafting require kids to follow detailed instructions to carry out someone else's idea. A craft has a starting point and an ending point. You're likely to hear, "I'm done!" in less time than it took you to set up the craft.

If you want your child to be invested in what they are working on, support them in their own ideas, not yours. They'll work longer and more industriously when they have creative freedom. Make it fun and interesting for them, simply by *not* telling them how to work with the materials. Following along with someone else's ideas usually isn't something kids look forward to.

Open-ended art—art without direction or structure—develops creativity, problem-solving skills, self-regulation skills, and understanding of emotions. And it's fun. When your child freely creates with art materials, they're building the skills that will serve them throughout life, from building frustration tolerance to finding creative solutions when things don't go as planned.

If you have a child who's "just not creative" or "doesn't like art," see what happens if you replace structured art activities with opportunities to get confident using basic art supplies paired with their own imagination, rather than from an instruction sheet or your ideas of what they could make.

But My Child Is a Perfectionist

Parents come to me about their four- or five-year-olds getting intensely frustrated with themselves. "They crumple up every drawing! What's going on?" If you are noticing some perfectionist tendencies in your four- or five-year-old, their brain is doing exactly what it should be doing. Around this age, your child's capacity to form a mental picture of what they want to create is much

FIVE WAYS TO REUSE OLD ARTWORK

- Tape a preschool painting down flat to the table. Odds are, your child created that painting standing up at the easel, so placing it down flat offers a new perspective. Take out some markers, stickers, or fresh paint. Allow your child to revisit their work and add to it.

- Use large drawings or paintings as wrapping paper. Kids love to gift their artwork this way, and this is a great way to do it. Let them have at it with a roll of tape and do the wrapping for you. It might not come out professional looking, but it's a great fine motor activity, and it will give your child a sense of pride.

- Recycle old artwork by cutting it into small shapes for a collage. Put out the pieces on a tray with glue and a piece of sturdy paper or cardboard and let your child make something new! It is amazing how these things turn out the second and third time around. Plus, you win, because your child is engaged in a non-screen activity and you didn't even buy anything!

- Post it! Mail that painting to a friend or grandparent. Brainstorm a list of people who might like to receive mail. Help your child fold their work and place it in an envelope. Show them how you address it, and let your child decorate the envelope. Head to the post office together and mail out the package, allowing your child to take the lead as much as possible. Boom. I just killed an entire morning for you! Your child and their grandparent will probably both be very happy.

• **Have your child choose a painting they remember making.** You know, that really special one that you can tell they spent ages on. Sit down with them and have them dictate a story about what is happening in the painting. It's okay if they make up something entirely new on the spot. It is the writing and sharing that matter here. Write down their words carefully (this is a great pre-reading exercise, by the way). Later that evening, allow your child to present their painting to the family while you read the story out loud.

greater than their hand's ability to follow through. It's similar to when they were learning to talk during their toddler years. They'd tantrum because they knew what they wanted, but they couldn't yet verbalize it.

Fours and fives can get very upset if what they are doing doesn't match the idea in their head or they feel like they aren't doing it well enough. The parental impulse is to say, "It's not a big deal, it's a beautiful drawing/painting/building/sculpture, honey, don't get upset," but the fact is that your child is upset. They don't believe you when you say their creation is "beautiful."

Here's a different way to support them as they work through this period of development. Say, "You're right, it won't look the same as in your head. Let's see if we can figure this out. Tell me more about what the monster you imagine looks like." Asking your child to describe their vision can help it feel more accessible. Ask questions like, "What is the shape of your monster?" Then encourage your child to implement their thoughts. "What kind of lines could you do to make that shape? What do the eyes look like, scary or friendly? What would scary eyes look like? Make your face look scary. What does that look like?"

If your child says, "I want to make a giraffe but I don't know how," start with the basics. "What does a giraffe look like? What kind of lines would look like that? What is the shape of a giraffe's body? What kind of lines would make that shape?"

You're not telling them how to do it, but you are helping them work through how to think about how to do it, one step at a time. You aren't doing it for them, but you are helping them work through how to do it themselves with support. This can apply to other situations where your child gets frustrated with not creating what they saw in their heads. If your child's block tower fell down, you wouldn't rebuild it for them. You would encourage them to think about why it fell down and problem-solve other ways to build it.

But My Child Doesn't Want to Get Dirty Hands

Many years ago, one of my best friends called me, absolutely distraught over her three-year-old son, who was developing an aversion to getting his hands dirty. He was never like this as a toddler. "What's going on," she said. "Should I call the pediatrician?" As a former preschool teacher, I had fielded many phone calls like this before. "They won't touch play dough!" "They cry if paint gets on their hands!"

Here's what's likely going on: Threes are becoming more aware of their bodies and how things feel in and on their bodies. They have a new sense of autonomy, especially with deciding to hold their pee and poop or let it go. They know how to express to you if something feels good, bad, or in between. Some children dive right into messy materials, while others need time to approach these sensations, and neither way is right or wrong.

The most interesting part of this, to me, is that the same kid who refuses to touch blue paint while fingerpainting will happily dig into the wet mud on the playground. Kids are a puzzle, but leaning into developmental norms can be very comforting for us adults.

When I taught three-year-olds, we put clay out for the kids to play with every day, and I had this one little boy who refused to touch the clay. He was very attached to me, and not yet comfortable being independent in the classroom. He was also at a developmental stage when he didn't want to get his hands dirty.

He had a lot of energy to expend, and he loved to kick and punch things. I knew he could benefit from working with clay because clay naturally invites that big physical energy—pounding, squishing, and smashing. So every day, I went over to the clay table and sat down, because I knew he would come sit by me to be near me. At first, I never touched the clay. I wanted to wait him out and mirror his presence.

Then one day, I just started lightly pounding on a lump of clay with my fist. He watched me for a while and walked away to look at a book. I did the same thing every day. Then at last, he started pounding on a lump of clay with his fist. Pretty soon, he was in the clay. He loved the clay. We punched the clay. We stomped on the clay. We did so much stuff with that clay, and it was wonderful!

What I did not do was go over to the clay table and say, "Here, try this! There's nothing bad about it. Just try it!" If I had done that, he probably would have resisted even more. The lesson here is to meet your child right where they are and start there. Don't direct them but if they are reluctant or don't have play confidence yet, set the stage or do a small thing they can mimic to get started. Whatever it is that they are resisting, ease in and be patient. With the child in my class who was reluctant to touch the clay, I eased him in by pounding the clay with my fist, not digging my whole hand in. You can show them what's possible without prodding them to participate. Let them come to it on their own terms.

This is really the point behind every play prompt and every independent play scenario that isn't going the way you planned. Do just enough to get them started and build their confidence that they really can play independently. They'll take it from there.

14

THE TOY CHAPTER

Have you ever spent money on a toy your child begged for, the one "everyone" was getting, and then no one played with it? Have you spent longer setting up a craft project than your kids spent engaging with it? Do you spend your child's independent playtime prying off play dough lids, fetching puzzles from the closet, and helping them read the directions on complicated toys? The problem isn't you or your kids. If you are nodding your head yes, this chapter will help you rethink toy selection, tweak your setup, and help you support sustained periods of true independent play.

Choosing and managing toys for your children doesn't have to be stressful, but it does involve some intentional planning. The wide variety of toys on the market, combined with wanting the best for your child's development, can make toy decisions difficult. One expert says this is the best toy. The next expert in your feed tells you absolutely not to buy that one because it will thwart your child's development. Now add in the loads of toys you previously purchased and the tons of gifts from well-meaning friends and family that are crowding you out of your own home. It's time to find a simpler, more sustainable approach to managing your child's toys.

The good news is that with small intentional steps, it is possible to get the toys under control and have some order in the chaos. It's possible to build a collection of open-ended toys that are just right for your child's personality and developmental stage. You can create a simple plan for what toys come in and what toys get stored away. Best of all, you can create uncluttered play spaces that your kids can walk right into and start playing without needing your help.

What Is a Toy?

First let's define what I mean by "toy." A toy is something your child plays with. It might be a figurine from your child's favorite show, or it might be a box of plain, unpainted wooden blocks. Stuffies, dolls, action figures, cars and trucks, tracks, and dollhouses are all obvious toys but so are materials like paint, paper, markers, and clay; metal pots and wooden spoons; child-sized cleaning items like brooms and mops, and small-sized yard tools like rakes and shovels. Play dough, yarn, pompoms, construction paper, scissors, sports equipment, child-sized ride-on vehicles like scooters, skates, trikes, and bikes—I consider all of these things to be toys.

There is a big difference between open-ended and closed-ended toys. An open-ended toy can be used in multiple ways with no "right" or "wrong" way to play. It tends to be simpler by design and supports different types of play as the child grows. The biggest difference between the two types of toys is that with an open-ended toy, your child determines how to use it, while a closed-ended toy has a specific purpose. Both types of toys can have a place in your child's playroom, but understanding the difference can help you choose toys that grow with your child and support creative, independent play.

For example, wooden blocks can become anything your child is interested in. A few unit blocks can transform into a cozy bed for dolls, part of a lengthy road for toy cars, a counter in a pretend store, or whatever it is that your child is "selling." Blocks can become a tall and complicated marble run or a house for dinosaurs. They are flexible props that support deep play that matches your child's interests and developmental stage.

A closed-ended toy is made to be used in one specific way—it teaches a certain skill or produces one specific end result. For example, a puzzle where pieces only fit together one way, or a shape sorter where the diamond block must go through the diamond-shaped hole. Some closed-ended toys, like an electronic rocket ship, might captivate your child during their space phase, but eventually lose their appeal, while other closed-ended toys, like puzzles and shape sorters, tend to hold lasting value. The key is choosing closed-ended toys thoughtfully.

I always lean toward open-ended toys because they grow with your child and support all possibilities for play. They work well for families with children of different ages—your toddler can stack blocks into a tower while your first grader uses the same blocks to create an elaborate building. Each child can play at their own level with the same blocks because the toy is able to meet your child where they are at that moment.

Good-quality open-ended toys can be more of an initial investment, but they will last for years to come. Our family built our collection gradually—starting with basic blocks and adding versatile items like play silks over time. A large part of our block collection is the same blocks I played with as a child. When you consider how long these materials last and how often they're used, they often prove more economical than cycling through more trendy toys. Think for a second about all of the plastic food, light-up gadgets, and remote-controlled vehicles that have made their way into your playroom. I bet if you added up the cost over the years, the initial investment in open-ended materials wouldn't seem as out of reach.

Curating Toys

Children naturally gravitate toward play spaces that feel organized, where they can easily find their favorite materials and have the physical space to use them. If your play area feels chaotic, you're not alone. The thought of sorting through everything can feel completely overwhelming. Most of us have stood in the center of the playroom wondering where to even begin. While open-ended toys create the foundation for meaningful play, your child's unique interests can be the focus as you decide what to keep accessible. As you curate, think about which materials have the capacity to reflect your child's unique interests and abilities.

For example, if your child is interested in vehicles, you should absolutely have vehicles in your playroom. Do they love horses? Great. Then horses should be a playroom staple. If they love to play with a big plastic kitchen, then keep the big plastic kitchen. Don't throw it out or give it away because you think it's ugly or takes up too much space, if your kids actually play with it. Is your little one crazy about Bluey? They can easily incorporate Bluey figures into their block buildings! However, you do not need to acquire every Bluey Playhouse and accessory, because that's when it becomes hard for them to imagine anything else and expand their play beyond what they see on the TV show.

Commercial toys like Paw Patrol pups, Barbie, and My Little Ponies have all shared playroom space with our blocks, balance boards, and magnetic tiles over the years. They've been loved and played with many different ways by many children. When you are choosing toys for your home, be intentional about the quality, quantity, and when too much is too much. When it comes to toys, less is more.

When building your child's play spaces, certain toys stand the test of time. While specific recommendations might vary with development, most items that I recommend will engage children from toddler years through tweens. Whether you are paring down or planning future gifts, there are some basic all-time favorite toys and materials my children have been using since they were small. These are also the toys and materials I most frequently recommend to clients. Here is a good basic list to create an inviting play space where your children can explore independently through open-ended play:

- **Magnetic tiles.** Magnetic tiles are a favorite for daily play in many homes. While typically recommended for ages three and up, even babies can play with them with careful supervision (always be mindful of choking hazards). Set a few tiles in front of your little one and watch them play by banging, clattering, and discovering. Their appeal spans years—even teenagers become engrossed in building impressive structures with these versatile toys. I keep a small set on our coffee table and everyone who comes over immediately starts tinkering.

SIGNS YOUR CHILD HAS TOO MANY TOYS

If your child seems overwhelmed during play, the culprit might be too many toys. Sometimes an overabundance of toys makes it hard for children to dive deep into play. The University of Toledo published a study in 2018 in *Infant Behavior and Development* called "The Influence of the Number of Toys in the Environment on Toddlers' Play." The researchers found that when toddlers have fewer toys available (four toys versus sixteen toys), they played for longer periods of time with each toy, they were more creative in their play, they found more ways to use each toy, and they had a higher-quality play experience overall. When they have fewer options, children tend to play more productively. It's similar to how adults can focus better in a tidy workspace.

Here are five signs that it may be time to reexamine the toy load in your home:

1. Your child seems to hesitate or freeze when choosing what to play with.

2. Play bounces quickly from toy to toy without settling into deeper engagement with one or two items.

3. Your child dumps out all the toys to find what they want (although dumping *can* be developmentally appropriate for young children).

4. Your child has difficulty cleaning up independently, because there is just too much.

5. Your child seems more relaxed and focused during play at places with fewer toys, like at the library or preschool.

I fully understand how tempting it is to buy it all, but as you shop, especially for the holidays, these are things to keep in mind.

- **Play silks.** Play silks are among those magical toys that can be adapted for any child. For babies, they offer sensory exploration with their silky feel and the way they sway with the breeze. They are a great toy for peekaboo and fit easily in a diaper bag for play on the go. As your child grows, these simple squares of fabric transform into superhero capes, flowing long hair, an obstacle to jump over, or a doll blanket. A collection of play silks and some clips replaces the need for a whole chest of dress-up clothes. I love how durable they are, too—a quick rinse and hang dry is all they need, even after water play at the beach or in the bath. When I think about toys that have earned their space in the playroom, play silks are always at the top of the list.

- **Unit blocks.** Much like magnetic tiles, we've been building our unit block collection for many, many years. Some of the blocks in our playroom are from my own childhood. Talk about heirloom toys! Unit blocks are wonderful, starting when your little one can sit unassisted. Build up a three-block tower and let them delight in pushing it down and building it again. Watch your growing toddler begin to stack tall towers and build enclosures for their dolls. The more they build, the more skilled they become. The toddler who once laid long flat roads for trains and cars grows into an older child who builds massive, complicated structures, challenging themselves to engineer new and different functions for their buildings.

- **Rocker board.** A rocker board meets your child at every stage. Babies discover they can crawl over its gentle curve, and toddlers delight in rolling balls up and down its slope. As your child develops, this simple curved board transforms into everything from a mountain for toy trucks to explore, to a swaying balance challenge that builds confidence and body awareness. Sometimes we'll flip it over, add a soft pillow, and it becomes the coziest spot for afternoon stories. It can be used as a lap desk, a low stool, or an extra seat in your playroom. It's amazing how one thoughtfully designed piece can support so many different kinds of play as your child grows.

- **People, animals, and vehicles.** Children play out the scenes and stories that encompass what they want to figure out, whether that's family life, animal adventures, or busy construction sites. A collection of these toys becomes the heart of countless play scenarios, especially when they're easily accessible in simple baskets. Your child will use them in block play, sand and water play, and all sorts of pretend play as your child grows and their interests evolve. They are also a good way for children to practice sorting and categorizing.

- **Play couch.** A play couch is a fantastic addition to any home with young children. It's incredibly versatile—perfect for building forts, creating obstacle courses, or simply lounging around. Ours has been used for everything from imaginative play scenarios to creating cozy play and sleep nooks. I love how the pieces are lightweight yet sturdy, allowing my kids to rearrange them independently.

- **Dollhouses.** A dollhouse is a powerful tool for helping children make sense of their world. A dollhouse can be big or small, and the most engaging ones are those that children can access from all sides, allowing them to move around freely as they work. Dollhouse play isn't just for girls; all children benefit from playing about their everyday life and the feelings that come with family life.

  For young children, less is more. A two-year-old doesn't need dollhouse furniture sets. They'll engage in deeper play with just a few simple people, basic small blocks, and fabric squares for blankets. Those are materials they can handle well, and they won't get caught up in trying to fit the furniture in the right place or get frustrated when their people don't fit on the bed and fall off. Instead, they can get right down to business and start playing. A dollhouse is the kind of toy that will grow with your family. As your kids grow and develop, add more furniture and accessories that are easier for older kids to handle.

  When space or budget is limited, a smaller dollhouse can work well. They can be found in thrift stores or on your neighborhood swap sites. What matters most is having a space where your child can explore their own stories. Place it where play naturally happens, whether that's in the playroom or right on your kitchen floor. A dollhouse grows with your family, supporting complex play as your children develop.

- **Play dough.** Watch children work with play dough and you'll notice something remarkable: They are completely absorbed in their work. There are no complicated directions, no lines to stay inside of, no prescribed tasks. In fact, play dough seems to be one of the last materials we still allow children to use without having our own agenda. Play dough offers our children a sensory learning experience that they can control. They get to decide how intensely to squish the dough or if they'd rather poke at it with a tool. They can go at their own pace and create on their own terms.

  There's a reason play dough has graced the presence of almost every good preschool program for decades. While children are playing, they are also exercising almost all areas of their brains. They are strengthening the muscles needed for writing, buttoning, and other fine motor skills. They're exploring math concepts as they take dough apart and put it back together, discovering ideas like "part to whole" and investigating shape awareness. Have you ever noticed how much your child chats while playing with play dough? They are telling their own stories and the stories of everything they're figuring out as they process the dough through their hands.

  One of my favorite things about play dough is its accessibility. You can make it together using simple ingredients or buy a few containers of it at the dollar store. Children can control exactly how they want to interact with it, whether that's pounding with a mallet or squishing or gentle poking with fingertips. When children explore materials on their own terms, that's when the best play happens.

COOKED PLAY DOUGH RECIPE

You could buy jars of brand-name play dough, but it's fun to make your own. Here is my recipe:

1 cup flour
½ cup salt
2 teaspoons cream of tartar
1 cup water
2 tablespoons oil
1 teaspoon food coloring

Combine 1 cup flour, ½ cup salt, and 2 teaspoons cream of tartar in a large saucepan. Gradually stir in 1 cup water mixed with 2 tablespoons oil and 1 teaspoon food coloring. Cook over medium to high heat, stirring constantly until a ball forms. Remove from heat, cool, and knead until smooth on wax paper. Store in an airtight container.

Mixed-Age Play Spaces and Safety

LEGOs are a choking hazard, scissors aren't safe around the baby, and the toddler keeps wrecking the preschooler's buildings. So what can you do about creating play spaces for siblings of different ages?

When you have kids at different developmental stages, creating safe play spaces can feel impossible. Thankfully, parents are some of the most creative individuals out there. We are always thinking on our feet, being flexible where needed, and coming up with solutions for the strangest of problems. Here are some real-life solutions that worked for my family.

I used to let my oldest sit up on the kitchen table—actually sitting on the table—to work on his LEGOs, while I set up the girls on the floor with DUPLOs. Think vertically. Do you have a high shelf that is only for the oldest, to store in-process projects?

Then there was a season when we moved the wooden blocks up to my son's room. He could shut the door, and his little sisters couldn't knock down his creations. It was perfectly natural for the girls to want to knock things down, *and* it was reasonable for him to want to protect his work.

When my sister had three little ones, she came up with another solution: She used a baby gate to surround her daughter's block area, keeping the little kids out of her older daughter's work while they were all in the same room together. Get creative, be flexible, and if it's not working, you can always change your mind and create a new plan.

Managing Messy Play

If the idea of mud play or finger paint makes you cringe, you are one of many. As a teacher and a mom, the social media posts that preach, "The little things don't matter, embrace messy play, your child needs it," make me want to pull my hair out.

Messy play can be valuable and important, *and* it can cause stress for families. I find the notion that parents should allow all messy play especially offensive to busy parents who do not have the bandwidth for a huge mess. I am offended on behalf of parents whose cultural upbringing tells them that neatness is a value to be upheld, and those who don't have the means for extra loads of laundry or stained clothing. If you don't want messy play experiences at your home, that is okay. There are plenty of other ways to enrich your child's play and learning.

If you're somewhere in the middle, know that you can incorporate sensory play while maintaining your home's cleanliness and your family's values and structure.

Bottom line, dealing with the mess of messy play is always going to be about front-loading. Here are a few guidelines that might help:

- **Why is doing this messy play activity important in the first place?** Get clear on this in your own mind. Otherwise, it's just going to feel like making a mess for mess's sake.

- **Set up your space with a physical boundary.** Use a canvas drop cloth to clearly define where messy play is and isn't allowed. Start by practicing non-messy activities on the drop cloth to help children learn the boundaries. Once they understand the limits, they can gradually move on to messier activities within this designated space.

- **Front-load your cleanup.** When planning a messy activity, set up cleanup stations on your drop cloth. Place a laundry basket for dirty clothes so kids can strip down right there, and keep a damp cloth nearby for wiping messy hands and feet before bathroom trips. Have a bucket of warm, soapy water ready for dirty tools like paintbrushes. This preparation means that when the play is over, messy clothes are contained, kids are clean-ish, and your tools are already soaking.

- **Only allow for messy play on days when you have the mental capacity.** If you feel like you are going to be irritated or micromanaging, or you feel like you cannot add to your mental load, don't do it on that day.

TOY ROTATION

When I scroll through social media, I am overwhelmed by watching parents caught up in elaborate toy rotation systems (keeping some toys out for play, others stored away, then rotating the fresh toys in and the used toys out on some schedule). Parents become so obsessed with perfecting a rotation system that they forget about following their child's lead. While scheduled toy rotation can be valuable, it's become yet another "should" in modern parenting.

Instead of maintaining complex rotation schedules, simply observe which toys gather dust and tuck them away or give them away. When play feels stale, spend five minutes swapping a few things out. Fewer toys paired with lots of unstructured playtime will nurture deeper, more focused play than any elaborate system you saw online. Do what feels best for you and your child because that's where you'll find consistency and success.

Guide to Gifts

Most parents, at one point or another, are overwhelmed by the onslaught of presents at the holidays and on birthdays, for their children and for other children. The toy landscape has certainly changed. When I was a child, toys came from Toys"R"Us or our local toy store. There were no toys to buy at the supermarket checkout or at the gas station. Target didn't exist, and big-box stores did not carry toys. As children, we only received toys for very special occasions.

Now, toys are everywhere, and children receive them what seems like all the time. Even teachers and coaches give out small toys as rewards. As parents, we can barely open a social media app without being served an ad and feeling like we need to buy this or that. When toys are constantly available, giving gifts at the holidays starts to feel extraneous.

Every year since 2018, I have published a gift guide, and I used to see this as something useful and fun. I wanted to help people find toys that were conducive to independent play and creativity. Now, it seems gift guides are everywhere in December—companies put them out, as well as influencers. Meanwhile, I've become a lot more hesitant to do that.

I saw a post the other day that said spending twenty-seven dollars a day adds up to ten thousand dollars every year. Now I can't stop thinking of all the parents who are spending too much on way too many toys for their children this holiday season, especially because all those toys are likely to stop kids from playing productively. I don't want to add to that. My mission is always to support parents and caregivers in fostering play for their children, so while parents ask for gift guides, I don't want you to overbuy for birthdays or over the holiday season. I don't want to contribute to the overconsumption of toys, especially when I know deep down that too many toys will *stop* your child from playing productively, completely defeating the purpose of my work.

Sometimes, of course, a gift is appropriate or desired, so when buying toys for the children in your life, my recommendation is to rely on basic, open-ended toys that will grow with your child, can be used in multiple ways, and are built to last both physically and developmentally. Would you rather your child have one wow moment when opening a new toy, or would you rather give them a toy they will play with for years? Instead of novelty, familiarity with an open-ended material can be used as a medium to explore their expressiveness.

This chapter is full of ideas for these kinds of toys. Remember, the goal isn't to fill your home, or the homes of friends and family, with toys. The goal is meaningful play. The best toy is the one a child actually loves to play with.

15

PREPPING FOR
A QUIET TIME ROUTINE

don't believe in parenting hacks. I believe in doing the work, putting in the effort, and understanding that things won't always go smoothly. But, if I had to choose one secret ingredient that will make your parenting feel easier and help you feel more grounded, it is quiet time. Quiet time is daily scheduled independent play where your child gets to do their own work while you take some much-needed time for yourself.

I've intentionally waited until now to talk about quiet time. When I first started teaching families, I did things a little differently. I used to have parents start with quiet time and then teach independent play skills. Over the years, I have learned that the opposite approach has better outcomes for families and children. When children learn how to play independently first, transitioning to a solid, quiet time routine is smoother for everyone.

Why Quiet Time Is Important

Why quiet time? Do you really need it?

The last decade has brought dramatic changes. As you know, screen time has increased. Demands on parents have intensified, and children have fewer opportunities to develop strong play skills. We wouldn't expect our child to swim across a pool without time spent learning swimming skills and building up the muscle strength and coordination they need. We wouldn't expect you, the parent, to cheer them on through the hard parts instead of rescuing them if they weren't prepared. If you saw them struggling, you'd jump in and save them! But, if your child was well trained for their swim across the pool, and you had their coach nearby assuring you that their struggle is safe, you'd happily root them on from the sideline.

Just like swimming, it would be hard for a child who is used to constant entertainment to suddenly switch to a quiet time routine where they are expected to play independently for thirty minutes. This is why I've saved quiet time for this chapter. Until now, I've been showing you how to teach your child to play independently by setting up your space, curating toys and materials, offering play prompts, etc. I've also been setting *you* up to support your child's independent play, not by ignoring them, but by creating an environment in which they can succeed, and keeping connected with them as they process changes, manage emotions, and want to celebrate their progress with you.

When independent play becomes more natural for your child, and you've become more comfortable stepping back, you'll both be ready for a quiet time routine.

You might be thinking: "My child is already playing independently—isn't that enough?" It can be, but if you want a scheduled break every day while your child is developing self-confidence, independence, and autonomy, then quiet time is probably for you. During quiet time, each child spends time alone—not next to you, not with siblings, not with screens, but alone in their room or play area.

Quiet time supports creative thinking and a strong sense of identity in your children. Children from babies to teens benefit from chances to take breaks, think, rest, and play. Everyone needs consistent opportunities for downtime, during which we can all get the time and space to rest, imagine, dream, and create. Everyone needs and deserves a break. All humans, at all stages of development, need to rest and recharge their minds and bodies. Regardless of your family's culture, personalities, interests, or beliefs, quiet time benefits everyone. It's also one of the best things you can do for yourself as an overworked, stressed-out parent.

For children, quiet time provides uninterrupted time to tune into their own thoughts and internal rhythms. It allows them to process their life experiences and to practice whatever they are working on. Have you ever noticed that after your baby goes through a particularly rough sleep transition, they develop a new skill, like sitting or walking? That's not a coincidence. A developmental leap causes interruption of sleep. I'm not a sleep expert, but to me, this little tidbit shows just how much extra time children need to process new experiences.

Quiet time is also crucial for developing self-regulation skills. When children have regular periods of calm, unstructured time, they learn to manage their own thoughts, emotions, and activities.

When children are learning new skills, quiet time gives them the opportunity to practice without prying eyes and unnecessary input from parents, teachers, or older siblings. Freedom from oversight allows children to build self-confidence. There is no need to be inhibited when you have this time to explore on your own. Instead, children can focus on what matters most to them.

Finally, and perhaps most importantly, *everyone's behavior is better when they've had some quiet, independent downtime.* Not only do children need time alone to decompress, but adults need it, too. While you may often need to get things done during your child's quiet time—work, cleaning, paying bills, taking a shower—it's important to remember that you, too, need some downtime to tend to your own physical and mental health. That's just as important as what your child needs and gets from quiet time. Getting a solid quiet time routine in place will take some work and determination, but it will make your family life easier in the long run.

Rethinking Boredom . . . Again

Let's circle back around to boredom before we get into the nuts and bolts of quiet time. Even if your child is getting good at independent play, the idea of a scheduled quiet time without siblings, friends, or screens may shock and appall your twenty-first-century child. Even if you haven't heard "But I'm bored!" in a while, you very well might hear it again when you first introduce quiet time. You might even start feeling guilty again. In this day and age, no-tech quiet time might even feel extreme to you. Let me assure you, and remind you, why boredom can play such a positive and pivotal role in your child's life and development.

It's natural for parents to worry whether dealing with the whining that comes with boredom is really worth it. *Will my child get into mischief? Am I somehow failing them by not keeping them constantly engaged?* Allowing space for boredom is how they will learn to use their own minds to find something meaningful to do.

I'll break this down and show you how to set limits and boundaries to support your children to use their boredom productively.

What will your child come up with if you don't come up with anything for them? You'll never know if you don't give them the chance to be bored. I encourage you to let go of the feeling that your child should be entertained 24-7, and instead, think about your own feelings about your child's boredom, which may be resurfacing when you begin to think about a structured quiet time.

How do you typically respond when your child complains of boredom? Imagine responding this way:

"You sound worried about being bored during quiet time. I hear you. And you know what? I'm not worried about it. It's okay for you to be bored, and it's okay for you to choose to do nothing and stay bored." These are your magic words to transferring the responsibility of figuring out boredom from you to your child, where it belongs. Don't worry—after quiet time, you're going to connect with your child meaningfully and fully, without ever having to "save them" from boredom.

When this becomes part of your routine with your child, it's amazing how free your child will feel to go off and create on their own. What your child really wants is for you to understand their struggle and make room for it. They don't necessarily want you to eliminate the struggle. They might not realize this themselves at first.

My friends make jokes about it, but I used to say to my kids, especially during the pandemic, "It's time for you to be outside." Sometimes they would sit outside of the glass door with their arms folded, pouting at me. I told them they could choose to sit there and protest, or be bored, or they could start playing, and it didn't matter to me either way. Eventually, they gave up pouting and learned that they really did have that choice—to have fun, or not. That became one of their most creative times, but they had to ride out the boredom first. They would figure out what to do, and it was always much better than whatever I might have told them to do if I was trying to control their play. They can't wait to tell me about it later—after the dishes are done or my meeting is over.

Here are seven important life skills your child will acquire when you let them get bored. Take a picture of this list on your phone so that you can have it handy when you're tempted to alleviate their boredom for them:

1. Boredom teaches your child to take initiative.
2. Boredom allows your child to develop a strong sense of self.
3. Boredom gives your child a brain break from overstimulation.
4. Boredom teaches flexibility.
5. Boredom teaches your child to become comfortable being alone with their own thoughts and ideas.
6. Boredom gives your child the opportunity to be curious and persevere without the shame of failure.
7. Boredom helps develop strong decision-making skills.

Quiet Time Motivation

Quiet time may sound great to you, but you may also be thinking, "There is no way my child will do that," or "That's not going to work in my home." If creating a consistent quiet time was easy, everyone would do it. No one would be relying on screens to catch their breath. No one would be running ragged and burning themselves out. This work will take consistency and follow-through, but I'm going to show you exactly how to do that.

The first thing I would like you to do is to get clear on your "why," before diving into anything that you truly want to work. This is absolutely key. You might be rolling your eyes at me right now, but skipping this step would be like driving on a windy road in the pouring rain without windshield wipers. Your why makes the path to your goal clear. When the storms come, and they will, you can turn on your windshield wipers by remembering your why, and you'll be able to see the road ahead again.

Even though quiet time can be a glorious time during which you are loved but not needed, you may still need more motivation. If you had the power to look into the future, what would you want it to look like in terms of quiet time? How would it benefit each family member? What qualities do you think your child might develop from having a quiet time? What skills might quiet time nurture? What might your child create? And what might you do with time to breathe, relax, catch up, or just meet your own needs for a little while each day? How would that change *your* life?

The skills and traits that grow from quiet time and independent play will support your child in becoming their most authentic self. They can own who they are and live according to their principles. Being intentional and doing the work to get structured with independent play will pay you back a million times over. Think about that. The impact of a consistent quiet time and independent play routine is powerful.

What Quiet Time Can Look Like for You

When my children were babies and not yet in any kind of school or childcare, I ran around like crazy all morning. The second I heard that first whimper from the crib, my feet hit the ground. I was on duty, feeding, dressing, diapering, preparing for an outing, going out, making sure no one fell asleep in the car because that would mean I'd blown naptime, and on and on.

When my two oldest were in school but my youngest was still home, I became intentional about taking a break during quiet time and investing in my own well-being, and my days began to look different. I could actually sit still and drink my hot coffee. Sometimes I stepped outside, or watched a show, or texted a friend. I usually ended up puttering around, which allowed me to have creative aha! moments. This is when I came up with my best ideas.

I was excited for when the big kids came home because I felt prepared mentally to respond versus react to their behavior. They became calmer and happier because I had the mental capacity to meet them where they were. I became much less moody, and the rest of the day would go more smoothly.

Even now, there are times when I do not take a break. I'll run around all day and crash at 3:00 p.m. Then I get cranky and short-tempered. The kids come home from school ready to connect, and I want to shut them out. I lack the energy to set up play prompts, or to even have any kind of conversation when I am driving them to activities. I don't feel like making dinner because my patience and energy are extremely low. Bedtime ends poorly. I go to bed feeling guilty. Maybe you know how that feels.

If you have already been working on independent play, you may have discovered that these feelings are getting better and the overwhelm happens less often (it's never going to disappear completely—that's just life). Quiet time can take this to the next level.

Think about (or write down) how your typical day looks when you don't take any time for yourself. Be really honest. How does it make you feel? What do you accomplish? How does it impact your interactions with family? Let your motivation to institute a regular quiet time in your home grow out of these thoughts.

The Quiet Time Rule Book

If you are ready to start a quiet time routine in your home, let's get down to how it works. While you'll have to adjust for your child's age and needs, there are three rules for a successful quiet time:

1. **Solo.** Your child plays independently, not with you or with siblings or friends.

2. **Screen-free.** Your child is free from screes, including phones, tablets, or television. Music or audiobooks are fine. (While screens have their place at other times, quiet time is not one of them.)

3. **Child-directed.** Your child takes the lead on their own play, meaning they get to decide what they will do with that time (within the boundaries of these rules).

These are nonnegotiable. Other guidelines (as discussed in the following three questions) are adaptable according to your situation.

Where should my child have quiet time?

While you are getting into the routine of quiet time, try to have it in the same spot every day. This will build a sense of routine and mastery for your child as they learn the mechanics of how it all works. Your child may begin to feel a sense of belonging or ownership over that spot, which will breed familiarity and build confidence.

When my children were young, and we still had a napping baby (or two!), quiet time took place in bedrooms. With the children safe in their bedrooms during quiet time, I was able to relax a bit. I could watch TV while folding laundry, listen to a podcast, or just close my eyes for a few minutes.

Many families live in smaller spaces where children have quiet time within sight of others. This is a common situation requiring some creative thinking. Can your child have quiet time in your bedroom with a special basket of toys they only use during this time? Or maybe they use the living room while you spend time in another space? If you do need to be where your child can see you, focus on establishing clear boundaries about interaction. Your child can learn that even though they can see you, this is still their quiet time.

How long should quiet time last?

The duration of quiet time is dependent on your child's age, stage, and temperament, as well as the limits you choose to set regarding timing. A short, successful quiet time is way more valuable than a long one spent crying and building negative feelings toward the idea of independent play.

Quiet time should be short at first, even just five or ten minutes when it is new. This sets them up for success. When children are successful with shorter quiet times, they'll develop the motivation to successfully sustain longer ones.

Watch for signs of readiness for expanding the length of quiet time. You might see more focus during play, better self-direction, or an eagerness for quiet time to begin. Try adding five or ten minutes to quiet times when things are going well. You'll know you've found your child's quiet time sweet spot when it starts to feel natural.

As they grow, you can increase the time even more. A four-year-old is much more likely to sustain a thirty-minute quiet time than a two-year-old. If they are prone to anxiety or slow to warm up, they might need even more time to build up to a longer quiet time. Also be flexible—sometimes quiet time will be a little longer or a little shorter, and that's fine, too. For many kids, you may eventually be able to work up to an hour.

When is quiet time over?

How will my child know when quiet time is over? Your child should have a signal that quiet time is over that doesn't come from you. You could use a timer, an okay-to-wake clock turning red, or when their music stops playing. The signal needs to come from this marker, not from you calling out or checking in, because the more you can remove yourself from being "in charge" of ending quiet time, the more successful it will be.

Similarly to using a picture chart for their morning routine, a signal lets them know what's coming so they can move through the routine with confidence. When the timer or clock is in charge of the ending, children can fully engage in their activities without constantly wondering, "Is Mom coming yet?" It will cut down on "Is quiet time over?" questions because you can deflect to the marker by saying, "Is your light on? That's when you'll know," instead of getting into a back-and-forth power struggle.

Technology Tip: If you have the technology to control your child's quiet time ending marker through Bluetooth, you can manipulate the quiet time to increase your child's success. If it's been forty minutes and technically the light is about to go on, but your child is very engaged in a pretend game, you can use your device to extend the quiet time by ten or fifteen more minutes without entering your child's space.

On the flip side, if your child is having a hard time getting engaged, and you know it's not going to be a long quiet time that day, you can make the light go on early. Shorten quiet time on that day and act delighted and surprised when they call you and tell you that the light is on and quiet time is over. Remember, your goal is to help your child build a positive relationship with quiet time, so use these adjustments thoughtfully to support their success.

Introducing the Concept of Quiet Time

If your child has never experienced quiet time before, here are some ways to bring quiet time into your daily routine in developmentally appropriate ways for babies, toddlers, preschoolers, and older children:

For Babies

Babies get loads of built-in quiet time because they take frequent naps, but it's still a good idea to start giving them opportunities for independent play right from the beginning. When your baby is calm and awake, put them in a safe spot, away from pets and siblings, for a few minutes at a time. They will likely enjoy gazing out the window or into a mirror. Some babies tolerate this beautifully for long periods, while some babies will tolerate only a few moments before wanting to be held. That's fine and has to do with your baby's personality. Either way, let them have that time, even if it seems short to you. As your baby grows, those periods of independent "play" will get longer.

Tip: If your baby is feeling fussy, try holding them and sitting quietly for a few moments. Slowly work toward short periods of independent awake time. If your baby protests when you put them down, wait a beat before you get them while lovingly reassuring them with your voice: "I hear you crying for me. You are safe. I'm right here and I am coming to hold you in a moment."

As your baby grows, you can start to set them down, even if they fuss. Rather than abandoning them, stay nearby, in eyesight. You can tell them out loud, "I'm right here. I hear you telling me that you would rather be held than down on the ground. I know this is different." It might feel silly, but you can even say, "We are practicing for quiet time when you grow older." Of course your child won't understand what you mean, but it will feel reassuring to you, and remind you of what you're really doing. Over time, your child will learn what those expectations and words mean.

Always supervise your baby.

For Toddlers

One way to introduce quiet time to your toddler is by offering brief periods of awake time in the crib to play. When they wake after a nap, don't rush in. Wait and let them stretch and relax. If they call for you, respond warmly by telling them you hear them, and they can play for a few minutes until you come get them. When you go to them, ask how their "quiet time" was so that they start to connect this play period with quiet time.

Setting aside time for quiet independent play when you already have a naptime built into your schedule is a jumping-off point as they begin to outgrow their nap. You are setting up time for them to practice playing independently. An important part of quiet time is that you are intentionally holding space for your child to practice playing. This timing will grow as they grow. Be very confident that your child can do this. If you are unsure, they will be, too. Build them up by starting small, to help you and your toddler feel successful.

Tip: If your child tends to be grumpy when they awake, try putting them in bed a few minutes earlier with a book and a soft toy so they can play on the front end of their nap. One of my kids wouldn't nap if they had a toy in their crib with them, so I would sneak in when they were sleeping and put a few board books and a soft toy to discover when they woke. It worked wonderfully to bridge us between naps and quiet time. Be creative. You know your child best.

If your child has recently dropped the nap and you are still fighting that whole "will they or won't they nap today" battle, you are in luck. If your child already understands the expectation that they go to their room and stay there for naptime, you can take advantage of this by giving them ownership in making quiet time a success.

Script: "I've noticed that your body is not getting tired every day at naptime. You only fall asleep some days, and that's okay. As children get older and learn about quiet time, they get to stay in their crib/bed/room and play all by themselves. You're getting to be a big kid like that. That means that you get to stay in your crib/bed/room and play all by yourself. *You* get to choose if you want to sleep or play. You are getting so grown-up that I am letting you decide!"

Giving a toddler ownership over naptime may feel counterproductive, but be confident in them. Give them time to practice and grow into it. They need to test limits and make mistakes because that is how they learn what quiet time is and that the same rules apply every single day.

For Preschoolers and Grade-Schoolers

If you haven't already established quiet times that grow out of naptime, and your child gave up napping ages ago, you can absolutely still introduce daily quiet time and build up their independent play skills.

Quiet time may feel completely unattainable if you've already settled into a different routine that is less than ideal for you, but I am here to tell you that I am positive you can do this. I have seen it happen for many families who felt it would be impossible. They did the work and used the skills I've shared in this book and in this chapter, and they are now enjoying their hour-plus-long breaks every single day.

You will have to build up to quiet time, though. Sometimes children will resist, but be patient, wait them out, and trust that what will happen on the other side of the whining or the tantrum is *so worth it* for them and for you. In fact, often the children who need quiet time the most are the ones who will fight it the hardest.

Understanding and maintaining the rules are especially important for them. Preschoolers and grade-schoolers are likely already in a routine of watching shows or having screen time every day so their grown-up can get a break, or so that a younger sibling can nap uninterrupted. Unlearning that routine and learning the new routine (especially the no-screens rule) is going to take some time and patience.

With preschoolers and older children, it's all in the finesse of the language you use. That is how you hook them in. Be genuine about how awesome it is to have your very own free time to be in charge of.

Script: "I want to teach you something new. It is something that older children and grown-ups do. It's called quiet time. Every day after our together time, it will be quiet time. That means you

221

will have your very own time to do your own activities. You get to choose what to play, and no one will interrupt you. Not me, not your brother, nor anyone else. You get your very own space and time to play LEGOs, draw, or build without anyone wrecking anything."

Your Quiet Time Mindset

No matter your child's age, no matter where your child has quiet time, you may still lack confidence in your family's ability to establish a successful quiet time routine. This is often a confusion about how to set a clear quiet time boundary your child can truly understand. How do you explain to your child that you are there in the house with them, maybe even in sight, but you are not available?

Setting boundaries is hard, but here is a technique that can help you set a clear and consistent boundary during quiet time. This isn't about forcing independence or controlling your child. It's about teaching your child that different times of day have different expectations. Use the language of "open" and "closed." This gives them a concrete picture of when you're available to engage with them and when you're not.

Script: "During quiet time, I am closed. That means I won't be able to answer questions or listen or tell you stories right now. When you're doing your quiet time, I'll be doing mine. You might forget sometimes and want to talk to me—that's okay! I'll just remind you that I am closed right now. When quiet time is over, I'll be open again, and we can share all about what we did during our quiet time."

Using "open" and "closed" to describe quiet time gives your

child clear language they can understand. When you say, "I'm closed during quiet time," your child knows exactly what to expect, unlike vague responses such as "Maybe later" that encourage repeated testing and questioning.

As Brené Brown reminds us, "Clear is kind. Unclear is unkind." And while being this direct with your child might feel uncomfortable at first, it's far softer than becoming frustrated and snapping at them when they keep asking. Children feel better when they don't have to guess at your mood or availability.

Developing a quiet time routine, like learning any new skill, takes practice. There will be starts and stops, successes and setbacks. Be gentle with your child and yourself through this process. You're both learning what works best for your family, and that path won't be a straight line from A to B. The limits you set and the time and patience you invest now will pay off when your child develops independent play skills.

16

IT'S QUIET TIME!

Are you ready to start your quiet time routine? We all feel a little better when we know what's coming, so prepare your child for quiet time by explaining what's coming. Be excited and positive about quiet time. If you are unsure about it, they will be, too. Explain that you will have some together time, and then you will each have a quiet time where you spend some time on your own. Then, assure them, you will have time together again right after; you'll get to spend some more time together telling each other what you did during your quiet time.

Here is how you might structure the process. This is just an example, which you can adapt to meet your family's needs and timing. More important than the actual steps is making the steps into a routine that works for your family.

Lunch or Snack Time

Giving your child a nourishing and satisfying meal or snack can be a surprising help for transitioning into a peaceful quiet time routine. When your child is full, their nervous system naturally shifts to a calmer state, creating the perfect moment to transition into quiet time. Take advantage of their biological response and set this up: Sit down together for lunch or a snack before quiet time starts. Reading a story while they eat will help them relax and stay at the table to eat enough. Knowing that your own adult time is coming makes it so much easier to stay present and unhurried during these meals.

Together Time

Together time is when you fill up your child both physically and emotionally. The more you fill them up, the more secure they will be. Think about together time as an assurance that you build a strong connection between you and your child before your separation for quiet time. When your child feels securely connected to you, they feel safe to disappear into a world of quiet time and independent play.

Here is how together time works. After your child has had their small meal or snack, explain to them that you will hang out with them for ten minutes. Set a timer together so that they will know when it starts and ends.

Tip: Allow your child to set the timer and press the buttons for you.

Put your phone and computer away in another room. Barring

an emergency, stay focused on the task and your child the whole ten minutes. No glancing at your phone! No jumping up when the dryer beeps. Do not be tempted to wash up the lunch dishes. Just sit and connect with your child. Read a book together, color, play a game. Or, give your child a choice of three things, such as looking at a family photo book together, working on a puzzle, or taking turns making up a story. If you have more than one child, it's okay to do this as a group, all connecting to each other.

Our lives rarely allow for us to spend an entire ten or fifteen minutes connecting with our children with zero interruptions. Even if you are home with your child all day, are you ever not multitasking? You will be amazed at the impact being fully present with your child can have. Really force yourself to be on their level. Make eye contact and physical contact. Be very present for these ten minutes.

I know this can feel awkward or uncomfortable if you aren't used to this kind of connection. Feeling this way is totally normal. Your child might feel it, too. That's okay and that feeling will pass when this time becomes a routine. Just remember, together time fills their bucket for when they will be playing independently in a few minutes. Remind them that when the timer sounds, it will be quiet time. Be visibly excited about it!

Script: "The timer will tell us when together time is over and quiet time starts."

Transition Time

The timer has beeped to end together time. Now it's time to transition into the main event! When this routine is still new for you, the transition from together time to quiet time might be bumpy.

Remember, it is natural for your child to test boundaries. You are not doing anything wrong if your child doesn't magically skip off to play independently for an hour. This takes time and practice, but you can do it! The more consistent quiet time is, the easier it will be. In fact, when your child does have a hard time making the transition at first, this is a good thing!

You can use their resistance as data to help you make a more informed transition tomorrow. You will take what didn't work and tweak it to work to your advantage during the transition. Use what you have and know about your child to smooth it over. This is another example of seeing your child's behavior as a form of communication about what you need.

Maybe today they say, "No, Mommy, I want to be with you, I want more together time." In response, tomorrow you could say, "Oh, the timer says we only have five minutes left. Yesterday you were worried we would run out of time. How do you want to spend those last five minutes?"

If your child is having a hard time separating, try saying, "Yesterday you were sad because you missed me at quiet time. Do you want to bring a picture of me into your room, or take my sweatshirt so you can cuddle with it while we are apart?" Or, "Yesterday we didn't have time to finish the puzzle during together time. Today let's do the puzzle on a tray so you can take it to your room and finish it during quiet time."

What you try might not always work, but the more you work with your child's resistance in creative ways, the more you reinforce your boundaries while remaining empathetic. When it's time, you can ease the transition:

Script, when timer beeps: "Oh, remember when I told you the timer would tell us when we could start our quiet time? There it goes! I am going to call Aunt Lisa back and fold the laundry during my quiet time. I'll tell you about what she says when quiet time is over. Maybe you will share with me what you were doing during your quiet time."

This takes the control off of you and puts it on the timer. Talking about your quiet time will invite them to begin thinking about their own, transitioning their thoughts to spending some time alone.

Quiet Time

It's finally time! For quiet time to be successful at first, especially if your child is still building independent play skills, you may need to give them a little boost at the beginning. Just as you personalized the play materials in your home and in the way you set out simple play prompts, you can personalize quiet time for your child with simple quiet time play prompts. They won't need these forever, but they can really help with children who aren't sure what to do during quiet time, or who say they "can't do it."

I want you to imagine for a moment that together time is just ending and you and your child are transitioning to quiet time. Your child is feeling apprehensive, and you need something engaging to encourage them. When children are first getting used to quiet time, an enticing invitation to play goes a long way. This is not a time to whip together an elaborate craft or hand them your phone, "just this once." Don't take too much time to set up an open-ended prompt compatible with your child's interests. Stay strong in your confidence that they can take your simple play prompt and go somewhere interesting with it. You want your time back for yourself, and your child needs the opportunity to get bored and creative.

There are other reasons why quiet time feels unsustainable.

QUIET TIME SHOULD NOT FEEL LIKE A PUNISHMENT

Even though you know quiet time is not a punishment, your child might feel like it is. Your kid is allowed to not like quiet time at first. For some kids, quiet time feels hard. It's uncomfortable and they don't like the initial difficulty. If your child is resisting quiet time, you might be inclined to say something like, "What do you mean? It will be great, it will be fun, you'll love it!" Instead, validate their feelings by saying something like, "You wish you didn't have quiet time today. That makes sense. It's new and you're still learning about quiet time."

If you suspect your child is worried or scared, gently say, "I wonder if you're feeling worried. Do you want to tell me more about that?" You can give them a special comfort object to help them feel more secure. You can say, "I'll be right outside and I'll check on you soon." Give them some choice, such as, "Do you want to be in charge of whether your door is open or closed?"

Some kids are simply not ready and they need more support. That is when you can step in and help ease the transition until their confidence grows. Start with very short periods and gradually build. Check in regularly at first. Celebrate small successes to build their confidence. The goal is to build positive associations with independence, and we do not want to cause distress.

For example, a friend's child was competitive and loved games. At first, they struggled with quiet time because games typically need other people. I suggested encouraging them to give their child simple materials to make up their own games. It worked! During quiet time, the child cut out paper pieces, wrote rules, created cards, and eventually built a whole library of games. Once we found that hook, the child was off and running.

Here are a few super simple ideas to get your child started when they need just a little boost to get playing. There is nothing special about these prompts—no list of materials or required directions. That is purposeful. I want you to recognize that you should make this very easy on yourself. Use what you have (and your knowledge of your child's age and ability to handle materials safely).

- **Random letters and numbers** around the house, like ABC magnets or wooden letter and number puzzles. Gather them up and put them out as a simple invitation to play.

- **A simple cutting tray** with scissors and things to cut will engage your child for long periods of time. Grab some materials from around the house (strips of lined paper, pieces of construction paper or patterned paper, pieces of yarn, even bits of junk mail that your child can easily and safely cut), and pop them on a tray. Done!

- **Crayons, a pencil, and some stickers that are easy to peel** (or start them by peeling up the corners), along with a few sheets of paper. Your little one can draw, stick, and color in whatever way they like.

- **A lump of play dough with buttons, toothpicks, and cut-up straws** are the bits and bobs I came up with. You can choose any enticing loose parts you find around the house. Add a little rolling pin and that's it.

WHAT IF THEY DON'T DO ANYTHING DURING QUIET TIME?

It is okay for your child to spend their quiet time however they choose, even if it looks to you like they aren't doing anything. They will likely tell you they are bored, which is a sign you are on the right track to creativity.

Your child might spend their quiet time lying on their bed, playing in a corner, or sprawled on the floor surrounded by all of their toys. While it may look like "nothing" to you, they are creating stories in their mind, softly singing to themselves, or processing their world. This kind of quiet mental play is just as valuable as more recognizable active, physical play. Allow your child to decide what kind of play they need.

Remember that you don't need to avoid boredom—you need to trust it. Giving your children time to do nothing can be the precursor to important growth. It might result in initial uncomfortable feelings and actions, but when you allow space for it, the other side of boredom is magical.

Closing the Loop

Your child just completed their first successful quiet time! Congratulations! Whether it was two minutes, five minutes, or forty-five minutes, you are on your way. Intentionally reconnect with your child in a way that honors how they spent their time.

Celebrating your child's wins in a way that is both meaningful and clear will build the self-confidence that your child needs for quiet, independent playtime. Here are different ways to reconnect:

- **Tell the story of how you spent your time apart:** "Let's tell each other about what we each did in quiet time today. I want to hear all about your time and share what I did, too!"

- **Notice the small details:** "You looked at books and played with dolls during quiet time. Tell me more about that!" or "I see that you put all the red blocks in one corner of your building and the green on the top."

- **Encourage growth:** "You've learned so much about quiet time. You stayed in your room until the green light came on, and you chose how to spend your time. Now we both have energy for the afternoon. Should we run errands or go to the park?"

- **View them as an expert:** "What is getting easier for you about quiet time? What feels tricky?"

Quiet Time Troubleshooting

Any parent knows that things don't always go as planned. Here are some common quiet time issues and ideas for solving them.

Lizzie, I'm telling you, they just won't do it!

When children strongly resist quiet time, they're usually communicating something beyond just not wanting to do it. Are they worried about separating? Are their independent play skills not strong enough yet? Getting curious about the "why" behind the behavior will guide you to adjust your approach and set them up for success.

Script (not when they are in the struggle, but later when everyone is calm): "Tell me more about your quiet time today. It was hard for you, and I want to learn more so that I can help you."

Script: "Today's quiet time was hard, and I want to make it feel easier for you tomorrow. Do you have any ideas of things that might make it feel easier for you?"

Script: "I noticed that you weren't sure what to play today at quiet time, and then you kept coming out of your room. I want to make it feel more fun tomorrow, so let's pick some new materials to put in your room for you to work with."

I still feel guilty about quiet time.

Many parents feel guilty about quiet time, even when it's going well. These feelings are so normal, and likely stem from messaging about perfect parenting, constant engagement, and enrichment. I hope by this point in the book, you are feeling more confident about parenting outside of social norms perpetuated by social media and the pressure to keep children constantly busy.

Quiet time is about giving your child the opportunity to develop self-direction through independent play. Again, you are not ignoring your child! Quiet time is also about becoming a parent who is refreshed and present. When you insist on downtime for all, you're modeling a crucial skill that your child will use their entire life. When the guilt creeps in, remember why you decided to invest in quiet time in the first place. Remember your "why."

What if they keep coming out of the room?

Just like with bedtime struggles, some children will test boundaries by coming out of the room or area during quiet time. When this happens, it's important to remain completely neutral. Calmly walk them back to their space. I know this is hard, but remember, it is your child's job to test limits, and it is your job to show them how limits work. There is a learning curve here, and you need to follow along. Don't give up! Many children will test you for a long time before it sticks. If your child is struggling, keep your language encouraging and quiet times brief.

Script: "The light is still pink in your room (or the music is still playing, etc.), and that means it is still quiet time. I will see you again when the light turns green."

Script: "You are still learning about quiet time. Sometimes when we're learning something new, it feels tricky. I'm going to walk you back to your room for quiet time. I can't wait to see you when quiet time is over!"

Another reason your child might keep coming out is that their space isn't set up for independent play success. Take a careful look at their quiet time area. Get down on the floor at their eye level and look around. Are materials safely within reach? Are the toys simple enough to use independently? Is the space overwhelming with too many choices? Ask yourself, if you were your child, would you want to play in this space? If the environment seems to be the problem, go back and review chapter 10.

Keep quiet time short in the beginning. Follow your child's cues, and end on a positive note. If you notice signs they're about to come out and they've been playing independently for a while, set off the timer before they reach for the door. This will be easier if you have a monitor and can see them in their space. When quiet time officially ends before they tried to end it—success! A win builds their confidence, and you can reinforce this after quiet time.

Script: "You played with LEGOs, you read some books, and did a puzzle during quiet time. Did you know you would be able to do so many things all by yourself?"

What if my child falls asleep during quiet time?

If your child falls asleep during quiet time, they likely need that rest. Trust their body's signals. Some children will consistently nap during quiet time while others may occasionally drift off.

Script: "Remember when you were little and you used to nap every day? Now you know how to choose whether you should sleep or play. You knew exactly what you needed today."

My kids really want to play together during quiet time. Why can't I let them?

It's great to have siblings who get along and want to play together. In many cases, siblings can be your child's most influential teachers. While siblings can and should play together at many other times during the day, quiet time is designed for solo play.

One of the core quiet time rules is that each child has their own space to explore and direct their own play. Solo play gives your child a chance to try out different ideas without a more dominant sibling influencing their choices. Plus, when siblings play together, they'll have arguments that need your help to resolve, which means you won't actually get your quiet time, either. Children learn to make independent decisions instead of relying on typical sibling dynamics. When children play alone, their play becomes deeper and more focused because they can immerse themselves at exactly the level they need. They don't have to negotiate or compromise. They can just play.

When quiet time ends, siblings get to come back together and share: "Look what I did!" and "I came up with a great idea . . ."

We stopped being consistent and now my child is resisting.

While you are still teaching yourself and your child the process of quiet time and independent play, staying consistent is very important to your success. That being said, getting off track is normal and expected, not a failure. Just like bedtime routines, there will be disruptions. The long-term goal is flexibility.

When you are ready to get back to quiet time, approach the routine with confidence. You already know what to do, and so does your child. Start where you are, take baby steps, and build back up to a longer quiet time. Remember your previous success, and trust that both of you will find your rhythm again. Getting off track is never the end of the road.

Script: "We are all feeling a little tired and cranky. We skipped quiet time when Grammie was visiting us for the week. We had so much fun watching movies, going to the zoo, and taking the train to the city! We haven't had quiet time in a whole week. I really need some alone time and I bet you do, too. Today, we will start quiet time again. Do you think you remember what to do? Help me remember the steps . . ."

We are traveling. Can we still have quiet time?
I don't want us to get out of practice.

When schedules are erratic, such as when your family travels, you and your child need quiet time more than ever. When meals are different, sleep is unhinged, and the routine is off, quiet time becomes an anchor.

Use whatever you have to work with to provide a safe, quiet-ish space for your child. Quiet time can be had under an umbrella on the beach, or on a chaise lounge at the pool. It can happen at Grandma's house, a hotel room, or really anywhere at all. Spread

HOW TO TRANSFORM A HOTEL ROOM
INTO AN INDEPENDENT PLAY SPACE

How do you have quiet time in a hotel room? The first thing I do when I get to any hotel is look for any baskets. There is usually at least one in the bathroom holding towels. Empty it out! Lay one large towel on the floor in the corner of the room. Set the empty basket on the towel, then fill the basket with a few of your child's favorite toys.

Show your child that this is their very own play space in the hotel! Designating a play space will invite lots of independent play. Add a pencil with the hotel pad of paper. Add in a few snacks like fruit pouches, granola bars, and a leak-proof water bottle.

When it's time for quiet time, your child will be set up to play. They can choose to go there, even when it's not quiet time. Having their very own space in this novel location feels interesting and gives them a boundary when the hotel room feels crowded. It might just spark entirely new play ideas for them.

a special blanket on the floor or set up a cozy corner in the hotel room. Use the timer on your smartphone for timing. You can even mix things up by using a new audiobook or music for listening on headphones.

Pack a special quiet time bag that only comes out during these moments. Include a few favorite books, simple art supplies like paper, clipboard and crayons, small travel toys, and a small towel or blanket to sit on. Keep the quiet time bag novel. The items are only for playing with during travel quiet time.

Quiet time away from home might look different and be shorter than usual. That's okay. Consistent quiet time, especially while on vacation, will provide a predictable moment of calm in the midst of travel changes and excitement. It will help you and your child feel more relaxed and more patient so that you can enjoy the trip. Stay flexible.

Script: "Remember when you were little and we had to go back to the hotel room for naptime? Now you're old enough to have quiet time at the pool. I'm going to sit right here and read my book for my quiet time. I wonder which material you will choose first for your quiet time."

Script: "Will you be in charge of telling me when the timer goes off and it is time for us to swim together?"

Quiet time might be tricky at first. It's hard to change your routine and build a new practice, but remember why it's worth it. Quiet time is advanced independent play, so when it's working smoothly in your home, despite the occasional bump in the road, you can feel confident that you and your child and your entire family have mastered the art of independent play.

17

SUPPORTING YOUR CHILD'S GROWING INDEPENDENCE— AND YOURS

This book is more like a cookbook than a baking book. Baking is an exact science, but cooking is an art. If you change an ingredient or measure wrong in baking, the product doesn't come out right, but when you're cooking, you have a lot more creative freedom. When it comes to independent play, measure with your heart and use the ingredients that appeal to you the most.

Your child's struggles and successes will continue to come and go. Rest assured knowing that by teaching your child the skill of independent play, you've built a foundation for much bigger things. The time you invest in independent play isn't just about keeping your child busy. It's about building the capability to focus and learn that will serve them their entire lives.

Even as someone who helps families with independent play and screen time daily, I still navigate these challenges. I've helped a lot of families integrate independent play into their homes. I've helped a lot of people manage screen time in their homes. Yet, my eleven-year-old still tries to negotiate with me about screens. No one will do this perfectly. When you're a parent, your job is never done. There's no finish line, and no one is handing out awards.

What you have here is a framework. This book and the strategies inside of it aren't meant to be a rigid collection of rules. See it as your sturdy collection of tools that you can reach for as you need them to build an independent play routine that works best for your family. As your child develops, come back and reread the sections that are relevant, and you'll find new strategies to adapt to current needs.

At the end of this book, I want to remind you that you don't have to reinvent your parenting to make this work for your family. Let this book lift you up, not overwhelm you with a perfectionist sketch of what independent play "should" look like at your house. This framework isn't about perfect parenting. It is about finding what works best for your child right now.

Your child will continue to say, "I'm bored!" sometimes, and that's normal, even in my house. When you hear those words, I hope you now feel confident that boredom is an important part of your child's life and take it as a sign you're doing something right. I hope you're walking away from this book feeling less overwhelmed because you've gained tools that make you feel capable. I hope you see yourself as the competent parent you've always been.

Your children will keep growing and changing. Nurturing their independence at every stage will always be worth your effort. Children thrive when they learn to do things for themselves, rather than learning that someone else will do things for them. This simple idea has guided me in raising my own three children, and I hope it will help you as well.

The more your child plays, the more their play skills will develop. Stay in the habit of observation so you can provide materials that grow with them. For instance, your child who spends a lot of time working with art materials will strengthen their fine motor skills and become more adept at managing tools. Support their growth by offering more advanced materials that match their developing abilities. If they're fascinated by a specific topic, visit the library for books that take them to the next level. Provide materials that reflect their growing interests so they can continue to play about what they're learning. When you stay connected to their play, you'll recognize what they need next.

Continue to stay present by listening and talking about your child's interests with them, whether it's soccer, Pokémon, or something completely unexpected. Your undivided attention shows them that what they care about matters to you. When you take time to learn about their inner world, even if it's not your personal interest, you strengthen your connection and support their confidence.

You will see, as time goes on, how independent play has fostered creativity, enhanced cognitive development, and built emotional regulation skills in your child. Their sense of self and confidence will continue to grow as they get better at entertaining themselves and handling challenges without constant adult guidance. Believe me when I tell you, the time you invest in supporting their independence will be rewarded many times over when you see your child flourish.

Watching my oldest child grow from infant to high school senior, I've witnessed firsthand how nurturing independence through a child-led approach can shape a child's development. We provided a supportive environment and a deep connection, but most importantly we trusted him to find his own way within it. Of course he's had ups and downs, but this approach has helped him succeed with our support, rather than relying on us to do things for him.

This past fall, as college application season arrived, we watched him tackle the process. While the parents of his peers were busy overseeing every detail, we were able to continue our practice of stepping back, trusting him, and offering support when he needed it. When acceptance letters started rolling in, I knocked and opened his bedroom door. The smell of teenage boy, sweaty sports uniforms, and cologne-scented body wash enveloped me. I looked at my boy and said, "You did this. You made this happen for yourself. I hope you feel that." His eyes reflected back to me his years of making small, independent decisions, and my years of sitting on my hands when I wanted to jump in and do things for him.

The road to this place hasn't been without bumps and potholes. There have been many struggles and setbacks along the way. But watching him grow into someone who we know can handle life's challenges and go after his dreams has reinforced our belief in giving children space to develop their own capabilities. His success comes not from helicopter parenting or ensuring he joined the "right" clubs and played the "right" sports. It comes from doing the opposite: stepping back and believing in him to find his own way.

When you step back so they can exercise their executive function skills and work through things in their own way through independent play and on into life, those skills get stronger. They get to practice regulating emotions when things don't go as planned. Every child has their own unique timeline for developing independence and will exercise that independence in different ways, using different strengths. Always look for your child's strengths. Give them opportunities to practice these skills now. The simple act of letting your child figure things out for themselves, whether it's a puzzle or managing boredom, builds the foundation for tackling bigger challenges later in life.

Supporting your child's independence can be uncomfortable.

As a parent, your natural instinct is to protect and help your child, but look for the sweet spot between offering support and stepping back. Allowing your child to work through manageable challenges is how you provide exactly what they need. Don't worry—they'll still need your guidance and support. You aren't going to leave them to figure everything out alone. Instead, be their home base. Stay close enough to offer support when needed, but back up enough to allow them to build confidence in their capabilities. The key is staying connected and scaffolding their growth instead of fixing things for them. Personality, developmental stage, and temperament all play a role here, of course, and one size most certainly does not fit all kids.

For most of us, worry is part of the parenting job description. If we want to raise confident kids, it is our job to work through our own self-doubt and anxieties. Your child will take their cues from you. Show trust in their abilities, and they'll learn to trust themselves. Sometimes the bravest thing we can do as parents is take a deep breath and step back.

When Your Child Is Struggling

I am well aware that trusting your child to navigate through struggles can be really hard. I know because I've been there. When we recently moved to a new state, it was a challenging transition for my daughter, who was in middle school. She was bullied badly during a fragile time, and she became depressed and anxious. It was the hardest season of parenting I have ever lived through. I watched my fearlessly confident child disappear into herself and for about fourteen months, I questioned my own parenting. Were my methods wrong? Was this somehow my fault? I spent a lot of hours in therapy, and digging into research about adolescence. Regardless of being a confident parent who is rooted deeply in my parenting values, I really started to worry I'd mishandled the situation.

Unfortunately, an inexperienced therapist and a lot of frustrated teachers were telling me things like, "You've got to crack the whip. She's not doing her work. She's failing. You have to punish her!" But in my gut, I knew they were wrong. Her depression and anxiety were making it impossible for her to study, rest, play sports, or connect with peers. No amount of punishing or bribing was going to make her get good grades. To be honest, I didn't care about her grades. I cared how she felt. I cared about her mental well-being and her ability to be herself.

It's very hard when therapists and teachers challenge your parenting. Well-meaning grandparents, aunts, uncles, and friends can make you doubt yourself. They'll tell you to push your child to play a sport they don't love because it looks good on an application, or force them to practice an instrument they hate. Trust your child. Make room for the things they care about and be there through the hard parts. When a child says something's wrong or shows you that something is wrong, believe them.

Today, I dropped off my formerly struggling middle schooler at high school. She is growing back her confidence, and her sparkle and fierce energy have returned. She is once again invested in her schoolwork and cares deeply about her friends and teammates. And you know what? She got back to that place while holding on to her core values. We didn't try to punish the anxiety out of her or demand that she quickly heal from trauma. We found an experienced therapist who could help her. We nurtured her while she healed. We held her up when she couldn't stand. We loved her and believed in her.

Of course you'll worry about how your child's behavior reflects on your parenting, especially when other people question how you are handling a situation. We've all felt that urgent need to control situations so that our child won't melt down in public. Sometimes we even go against our own values so we look better to others. It takes time and experience to accept that your child isn't programmed to behave perfectly and that you won't ever parent perfectly, either. No one parents the way they want to all the time. Think of it as the 80/20 rule. Aim to parent in a way that is aligned with your values most of the time, and forgive yourself the rest.

Sometimes good parenting feels bad. Sometimes it's really hard to say no to your child, to set boundaries, and to be the parent in the room whose child isn't like the other children. Our society is focused on measurable achievements—grades, awards, extracurriculars—and it's hard to trust that supporting self-discovery has deeper value. Stick with your values. You have intentionally and consciously identified them, and deep in your heart, you know that parenting according to those values is what is best for your child.

Training your brain to approach parenting with openness and curiosity sets the foundation for connection as your child struggles and grows. When they enter their teen years, you'll have a one-dimensional view of what's happening in their world, and believe me, there's so much more beneath the surface. If you respond with quick judgments instead of genuine curiosity, your child will share less and less and you will miss half the picture. Lead with openness and let that signal that it's safe to be honest with you.

When You Are Struggling

It's hard to say no when saying yes would be so much easier. It's hard not to let your own fear, guilt, anxiety, or self-doubt creep in when making parenting decisions or interacting with your kids. Sometimes we are so overwhelmed ourselves that we cave because we just can't handle another moment of chaos. We all have times when there's no bandwidth to stick with the plan, and that's okay.

Aligned parenting looks different for everyone. Parenting through my daughter's depression and anxiety gave me a whole new insight into parenting through a crisis. That kind of stress leaks out into the entire family. During that time, my youngest child watched more TV than she ever had before because I just couldn't deal with anything else, and I am okay with that. It was what worked for us at the time. When you are in a hard season, it is okay to take shortcuts.

Sometimes the only quiet moment you'll get is after bedtime, and that's okay, too. Don't add unattainable self-care "shoulds" to your mental load. Whether it's fifteen minutes to drink your coffee alone, a quick walk around the block, or an hour to do something just for you, take those moments when they come, but don't feel they are an obligation. You know that advice to new moms, "Sleep when the baby sleeps?" So unhelpful. Life often doesn't comply with your needs for self-care or a nap. You do need breathing room, just as much as your child needs independent play. Look for it, and take it where you can. And if you're wrestling with anxiety or depression, know that you aren't alone. All parents struggle, and getting support can make a real difference for your entire family.

Here are some final reminders that I hope you will take with you.

INDEPENDENT PLAY TAKEAWAYS

1. Start where you are. If independent play is new and challenging, start small and short.

2. Observe your child's play without intervening.

3. Pause before rushing in to fix problems and alleviate difficulties.

4. Stay flexible in your definition of play. Play can look like many things.

5. When connecting and commenting on play, keep it neutral. Narrate or recount without praise or correction.

6. Acknowledge your child's feelings without judging, no matter what they are. All feelings are okay, but you can still set limits around behavior.

7. Intentionally create space for boredom.

8. Connect before and after independent play to build confidence and security. Close the loop.

9. Model your values to your children.

10. Take care of your own needs.

The last thing I will say about independent play is that it is like a form of meditation. It is an ongoing practice. Meditation looks so different for everyone. It is personalized. People have a vision of what it's supposed to look like, but those who are well practiced do it in many ways.

In meditation, you can have the perfect setup and environment to do it, but you want to be able to do it anywhere. You want to be able to access that sense of inner calm and centeredness, that sense of getting in touch with yourself, and that feeling that you can self-regulate. When you do it regularly, meditation helps you give yourself what you need. And yes, while anyone can do it, the people who practice and commit to it are the people who go deep with it, and it impacts their entire life.

Independent play is the same. It is personalized. It doesn't necessarily look how everyone thinks it should look. It helps to calm and soothe. It helps everyone get back in touch with themselves and regulate their emotions. Independent play gives you and your child what you need, and if you practice and commit to it, it will change your family's life. If you value it and tend to it, the skill of independent play will be with your child forever.

ACKNOWLEDGMENTS

If only my younger self could see me now. We wrote a book! I struggled in school and spent most of my time hoping no one would call on me or catch on to the fact that I was completely and utterly lost. I still have nightmares about overdue homework and failed tests, and I think that's why I became a teacher—to meet children where they are, accept them, and help them see themselves as capable and important.

This book wouldn't exist without the many people who have shaped both my journey and my philosophy along the way. I'm deeply grateful to each of you. Thank you to all the incredible children who have come through my life and shown me who they are. Thank you to the mentors and teachers I have had the privilege of learning from at the Bank Street College of Education and at the Downtown Little School. At the time I didn't know it, but you've impacted so much of who I am and how I show up in the world today.

Thank you to Alex Glass, my agent, who helped me see that it was time to put this book into the world, and that I was completely capable of doing so. Eve Adamson, my writing partner, thank you for holding my hand and never letting go the entire way through. Michelle Howry, my editor, I knew you understood this project from our first conversation. I am forever grateful for your warmth and encouragement. Thanks for taking a chance on me. Ashley Di Dio and the entire team at Putnam who brought this project to life, thank you as well for helping to make this book happen.

Thanks to Meri Cherry, my very first online friend, who inspires me always, and to Devon Canastra, who has supported my work since the basement days of The Workspace for Children. You are an incredible friend, and I couldn't do this work without having you on the other end of the line.

Thanks to my mom, who gave us endless opportunities to play and create throughout our childhoods. To my late father-in-law, Abe, who was my biggest supporter. From water tables to block shelves, if I could dream it, he could build it. And to Dave's mom, who always listened closely, letting me find my way without judgment. We miss you guys every day.

I must thank my husband and partner in everything, Dave. There was never a moment of hesitation when I shared the idea of The Workspace for Children with you. You were all in. Your total confidence in me scares me sometimes, but here we are!

What would this book be without my children, Nate, Ruby, and Sloane? You have taught me more about the importance of play than any book, statistic, or workshop ever will. The memories of you playing on the beach, in the playroom, and in our backyard, the whispered pretend games, the paint splatters, adventures in the woods, and the sheer chaos of it all is the movie in my mind that I will never stop watching on repeat. Continue to navigate through the world in a way that is all your own, because that is your gift. Your uniqueness.

And last but certainly not least, thank you to every single member of The Workspace for Children community. Thank you for growing up with me and parenting alongside me.

This book is for every parent who is brave enough to see their child for who they are rather than who society wants them to be.

APPENDIX: RESOURCES

My Favorite Age-Appropriate Toys

These are general recommendations that you can adapt to your own child's needs, preferences, and developmental stage. Many of these toys interweave and build on one another, offering new possibilities as your child grows. A block that starts as a simple stacking toy for a toddler will become part of complex buildings years later. If your child enjoys toys that are listed for ages younger or older than they are, that's wonderful—these ages are estimates for when and how these toys will be useful and engaging for children. Please see these as guidelines, not rules. I have repeats here because so many open-ended toys remain fun, useful, and appropriate for a wide variety of ages.

Infant to 3 Months

- High-contrast black-and-white cards or soft books
- Unbreakable baby mirrors
- Simple rattles
- Play silks
- Soft lovey

3 to 6 Months

- Soft textured balls that are easy to grasp
- Silicone teething toys with different textures
- Musical toys that respond to touch

6 to 9 Months

- Stacking cups or soft blocks
- Simple pop-up toys
- Large connecting rings

9 to 12 Months

- Push-and-pull toys that encourage crawling and walking
- Board books with thick pages

12 to 24 Months

- Push-and-pull walking toys with sturdy bases
- Ride-on toys
- Large, soft balls
- Climbing structures scaled for toddlers
- Large wooden blocks
- Simple puzzles (3–4 pieces)
- Large threading beads with thick string
- Short chunky crayons and thick paper
- Simple dress-up items, scarves, and play silks
- Child-sized household items (play phone, brush, cups)
- Soft dolls or stuffed animals
- Simple play food items

- Board books with simple stories and clear pictures
- Nesting and sorting toys

2-Year-Olds

- Play kitchen
- Simple props (doctor kit)
- Dolls and stuffed animals
- Playhouse or tent
- Play couch
- Magnetic tiles
- Kitchen helper or learning tower
- Blocks
- Small world items (figures, vehicles, animals)

3-Year-Olds

- Unit blocks
- Magnetic tiles
- Play couch
- Art materials (play dough, paint, large crayons)
- Loose-parts collection (wood pieces, large buttons, fabric scraps, natural items)
- Dress-up materials (fabric pieces, simple costumes, accessories)
- Small world items (figures, vehicles, animals)
- Building materials (cardboard boxes, paper tubes)

4-Year-Olds

- Unit blocks
- Magnetic tiles

- Light table
- Art supplies (markers, scissors, tape, collage materials)
- Play silks
- Small world materials (variety of figures, dependent on interests)
- Play couch
- Large construction items (boxes, fabric, clips)
- Board games and card games (simple rules, turn-taking)
- Science and nature tools (magnifying glass, tweezers, collection jars)
- Pattern blocks and manipulatives
- Writing and drawing tools and paper varieties
- Indoor movement equipment (balance beam, stepping stones)
- Sensory materials (kinetic sand, play dough)
- Construction sets with moving parts (gears, nuts and bolts, linking pieces)
- Small building materials (simple LEGO sets)

5-Year-Olds

- Unit blocks
- Construction sets (LEGO, gears)
- Art materials (real tools, variety of papers, clay)
- Complex games (strategy, memory, cooperative)
- Science equipment (microscope, measurement tools)
- Writing and drawing materials (variety of tools, blank books, paper)
- Advanced building sets (magnetic tiles, marble runs)
- Small world collections (multiple themes dependent on interests, loose parts)
- Play silks with clips

- Light table
- Pattern-making materials (beads, tiles, weaving materials)
- Engineering materials (pulleys)
- Fine motor materials (beading, sewing)
- Play couch

6-Year-Olds

- Construction sets (LEGO, snap circuits, marble runs)
- Art supplies
- Complex strategy games (chess)
- Writing and publishing station (paper types, staplers, tape)
- Creation supplies (tape, tools, recyclables, wood)
- Play silks and clips
- Math manipulatives (geometric shapes, measuring tools)
- Handcrafting supplies (weaving, sewing, woodworking)

7- and 8-Year-Olds

- Complex construction (LEGO Technic, K'Nex, architecture sets)
- Magnetic tiles
- Unit blocks
- Play silks
- Maker space materials (real tools, wood, fabric)
- Art and design materials (graph paper, rulers, 3D materials)
- Strategy games (Catan Junior, Ticket to Ride, chess)
- Creative-writing tools (journals, blank books)
- Real-world tools (measuring, cooking)
- Building (rope, clips, pulleys)
- Handcrafts (knitting, beading, woodworking)

9- and 10-Year-Olds

- Complex building systems (advanced LEGO)
- Maker space supplies (real tools)
- Strategy games (complex rules, long-term campaigns)
- Handcrafts (detailed projects, quality materials)
- Real-world tools (cooking, gardening, building)
- Special interest deep dive materials (based on interests)

Parenting Books

These are some of the books I've found most useful for parents—they come from many different perspectives and cover a wide variety of parenting issues.

Good Inside: A Guide to Becoming the Parent You Want to Be by Dr. Becky Kennedy

Elevating Child Care: A Guide to Respectful Parenting by Janet Lansbury

Free to Learn: Why Unleashing the Instinct to Play Will Make Our Children Happier, More Self-Reliant, and Better Students for Life by Peter Gray

The Power of Play: Learning What Comes Naturally by David Elkind, PhD

How to Talk So Kids Will Listen & Listen So Kids Will Talk by Adele Faber and Elaine Mazlish

The Whole-Brain Child by Daniel J. Siegel, MD, and Tina Payne Bryson, PhD

Peaceful Parent, Happy Kids by Dr. Laura Markham

Hunt, Gather, Parent by Michaeleen Doucleff

Your One-Year-Old: The Fun-Loving, Fussy 12- to 24-Month-Old by Louise Bates Ames, PhD; Frances L. Ilg, MD; and Carol Chase Haber, MA

Your Two-Year-Old: Terrible or Tender by Louise Bates Ames, PhD, and Frances L. Ilg, MD

Your Three-Year-Old: Friend or Enemy by Louise Bates Ames, PhD, and Frances L. Ilg, MD

Your Four-Year-Old: Wild and Wonderful by Louise Bates Ames, PhD, and Frances L. Ilg, MD

Your Five-Year-Old: Sunny and Serene by Louise Bates Ames, PhD, and Frances L. Ilg, MD

Your Six-Year-Old: Loving and Defiant by Louise Bates Ames, PhD, and Frances L. Ilg, MD

Your Seven-Year-Old: Life in a Minor Key by Louise Bates Ames, PhD, and Carole Chase Haber, MA

Your Eight-Year-Old: Lively and Outgoing by Louise Bates Ames, PhD, and Carole Chase Haber, MA

Your Nine-Year-Old: Thoughtful and Mysterious by Louise Bates Ames, PhD, and Carole Chase Haber, MA

Your Ten- to Fourteen-Year-Old by Louise Bates Ames, PhD; Frances L. Ilg, MD; and Sidney M. Baker, MD

Links to My eBooks

Looking for more from me? Here are some ebooks you can find on my website, workspaceforchildren.com.

A Parent's Handbook for Starting School: https://www.workspace forchildren.com/parents-handbook-to-starting-school

The Hitting Handbook: https://www.workspaceforchildren.com/the
-hitting-handbook

Block Play Simplified: https://www.workspaceforchildren.com/block
-play-simplified

The Play Plan: https://www.workspaceforchildren.com/the-play-plan

The Big Kid Play Plan: https://www.workspaceforchildren.com/the
-play-plan-big-kid-edition

The "I Wish I Knew This Sooner" Guide to Magnetic Tiles: https://work
space-for-children.kit.com/ca5cdf71b9

NOTES

7 **Loris Malaguzzi, the founder:** For more information, see https://www
.reggiochildren.it/en/reggio-emilia-approach.

17 **A *New York Times* headline published during the pandemic quarantine:** Alexis Soloski, "How to Entertain Your Kids This Summer? Maybe
Don't," *New York Times*, June 18, 2020, https://www.nytimes.com/2020
/06/18/arts/kids-summer-activities-virus.html.

17 **Another *NYT* article around the same time:** Kate Rope, "Now's a Good
Time to Teach Your Kids to Play on Their Own," *New York Times*, April 3,
2020, https://www.nytimes.com/2020/04/03/parenting/kids-indepen
dent-play-coronavirus-quarantine.html.

59 **It is the child's job to create:** Kenneth R. Ginsburg, "The Importance of
Play in Promoting Healthy Child Development and Maintaining Strong
Parent-Child Bonds," *Pediatrics* 119, no. 1 (2007): 182–91, https://doi.org
/10.1542/peds.2006-2697.

105 **Parenting expert Janet Lansbury:** "5 Benefits of Sportscasting Our
Child's Struggles," Janet Lansbury, April 25, 2013, https://www.janetlans
bury.com/2013/04/5-benefits-of-sportscasting-your-childs-struggles.

119 **High levels of parental stress are associated:** Diane Seguin et al.,
"School's Out: Parenting Stress and Screen Time Use in School-Age Chil-
dren During the COVID-19 Pandemic," *Journal of Affective Disorders
Reports* 6, 100217 (2021), https://doi.org/10.1016/j.jadr.2021.100217.

184 **Research supports this—a 2014 study:** Jane E. Barker et al., "Less-
Structured Time in Children's Daily Lives Predicts Self-Directed Ex-

ecutive Functioning," *Frontiers in Psychology* 5 (2014), https://doi.org /10.3389/fpsyg.2014.00593.

196 **The University of Toledo published:** Carly Dauch, "The Influence of the Number of Toys in the Environment on Toddlers' Play," *Infant Behavior and Development* 50 (2018): 78–87, https://doi.org/10.1016/j.infbeh .2017.11.005.

INDEX

Note: Italicized page numbers indicate material in photographs or illustrations.

ABOUT THE AUTHOR

Lizzie Assa, MSEd, is the founder of The Workspace for Children and head of play and development at Lalo. She is also a parenting strategist, play expert, and mother of three. With a background in early childhood education and experience working with families and children, Lizzie helps parents and caregivers avoid burnout by teaching their children independent play. She is a firm believer in the power of simplicity and consistency in play and is dedicated to promoting these values. Prior to starting The Workspace for Children, Assa received an MSEd from the Bank Street College of Education in New York City and taught nursery school at Downtown Little School and then the City and Country School in Manhattan. She has been featured in various publications such as *Parents* magazine, *NYT Parenting, Time,* and *The Wall Street Journal.*

Connect with Lizzie Assa Online

WorkspaceForChildren.com
�facebook ⊙instagram TheWorkspaceForChildren

2 04